Arguments for Socialism

Series editor: John Harrison

Arguments for Socialism is a new series of popular and provocative books which deal with the economic and political crisis in Britain today. The series argues the need for a radical rethinking of major political questions and contributes to the debates on strategy for the left.

'One of the main reasons why the Tories swept to power in 1979 was that the Labour movement had over the years almost ceased to argue for socialism. This new series, *Arguments for Socialism*, can play a significant part in re-establishing the necessity for a socialism that is democratic, libertarian and humane.' *Tony Benn*

It Makes You Sick

The Politics of the NHS

Colin Thunhurst

Pluto Press

First published 1982 by Pluto Press Limited,
Unit 10 Spencer Court,
7 Chalcot Road,
London NW1 8LH

British Library Cataloguing in Publication Data
Thunhurst, C.   It makes you sick.—(Arguments for socialism)
1. Great Britain—National Health Service
I. Title   II. Series
362.1'0941   RA395.G6
ISBN 0 86104 503 3

Designed by Clive Challis A Gr R
Typeset by Promenade Graphics Limited,
Block 23a Lansdown Industrial Estate, Cheltenham GL51 8PL
Printed and bound in Great Britain
by Richard Clay (The Chaucer Press) Ltd, Bungay, Suffolk

Dedication

To
Cecil Foggitt, Kay Habeshaw, Jessie Vaughan
Horace Windle and Nellie Windle
and to
any other five people who
have between them given over 250 years
to the socialist movement

Contents

Acknowledgements

This book is a product of arguments and discussions that have gone on for a number of years in the radical science and radical health movements. In particular it owes most to the existence and collective experiences of the British Society for Social Responsibility in Science and the Politics of Health Group. It is wrong to single out individuals, but this might be the only opportunity that I'll get to thank Lucy Craig, Gordon Best, Gillian Elinor and Jonathan Rosenhead for many years friendship, many hours conversation and many nights sleeping space.

A number of people commented on parts or on the whole of the manuscript at various stages. I am particularly grateful to Mick Carpenter, Lesley Doyal, Jane Greetham, Tom Heller and Jude Windle, and can only apologise that the publishers' tight schedule left no opportunity to do their valuable comments justice. The same tight schedule left Kate Holman with more than the normal problems of working on a manuscript. Cecil Foggit, Kay Habeshaw, Jessie Vaughan, Horace Windle and Nellie Windle generously gave their time and reminiscences. Lyn Mansfield offered much valued advice, support and encouragement throughout a very hectic period.

1.

Introduction

Before the National Health Service

I was born on 6 August 1948—one month, and a day, after what has been called 'The Appointed Day'—the day upon which the British National Health Service came into existence. I was born into the National Health Service and I have lived all my life within the National Health Service. Official estimates of the age distribution of the British population suggest that people born since the foundation of the NHS, like myself, now form a majority of the population of this country.

Thus, over half the people now living under the NHS will have no personal recollection of life, health and ill-health without it. And if you also add in all the people who would have been too young in 1948 to have their own recollections, it becomes apparent that the numbers of people who can remember much about life before the NHS now form quite a clear minority—and one, of course, which is steadily shrinking.

This is a book about the National Health Service. Primarily I will be arguing that it has 'failed to deliver the goods'—indeed, that there is no way that, within the social, political and economic framework under which we live, it could have done so. But in advancing this argument I do not want to lose sight of the extent to which the NHS *has* benefited ordinary working people; how conditions now are better than forty, fifty or more years ago.

Having no recollections of my own of life in the 1920s, 30s and 40s I decided to speak to some people who do. Cecil Foggitt, Kay Habeshaw, Jessie Vaughan, Horace Windle and Nellie Windle have all been involved in the socialist movement in Sheffield for over 50 years. They have a wealth of experiences dating from before the creation of the National Health Service which they willingly shared with me.

Cecil Foggitt   Cecil Foggitt qualified from medical school in 1941. After being demobilised from the army in 1946 he did a brief spell of training as a house surgeon in two Sheffield hospitals until the end of the year. On 1 December 1946 he entered general practice, in which he worked in various areas of Sheffield until his recent retirement.

Cecil Foggitt has been a fervent believer in the NHS and a member of the Socialist Medical Association (now the Socialist Health Association) throughout this period. He was in the unenviable position of being among the small minority of medical practitioners who were prepared to argue the virtues of a National Health Service to their colleagues prior to its foundation. He admits to approaching this task with a certain relish, having gained sufficient experience of the iniquities of health care provision under the previous patchwork system.

Cecil told me of the contrasting hospitals that existed before 1948: the difference between the quality of medical care that was available in the voluntary and in the municipal hospitals. The prestige of the former lay in the fact that they were under the charge of consultants who offered their services voluntarily, gaining their income from undertaking private practice. Beneath them were paid junior medical staff working for the experience. The municipal hospitals were serviced by full-time salaried staff, and specialist services were only made available by special arrangement. Cecil spoke of the marvellous work that was done by a number of his colleagues in the municipal hospital who never enjoyed the limelight nor the financial return of their counterparts in the voluntary sector. Despite their efforts, the options for care and treatment that they were able to offer patients were of a markedly inferior quality. The voluntary hospitals were charitable institutions which accepted patients at the discretion of the consultants. These would sometimes be the poorer people, though they normally gained their hospital care from the municipal sector.

Cecil also outlined the inequalities of general practice. 'Panel doctors' were paid on a per capita basis for employees who received less than a specified wage. This system of insurance funding didn't cover the children or other dependents of workers. They only received treatment on a private basis being sometimes covered by separate insurance schemes. The cost of treatment varied from practice to practice. In the practice in which he worked Cecil recalled that the charges were 4s 6d (22½p) or 5s (25p) for a home visit and 2s 6d

(12½p) for a visit to the surgery. Doctors elsewhere could charge much more. Poor Law coverage was available for people who could prove that they didn't have any money; but as general practitioners only earned 1s 3d (6¼p) for each consultation, they did not encourage Poor Law patients. Cecil had no doubt that these payments deterred patients.

In terms of the medical conditions encountered, the general practitioners' work was also different from now. Cecil recollected that in the area in which he practised at the time—Attercliffe in Sheffield's East End which housed the heavy industry of the Don Valley and the workforce which operated it—bronchitis was a way of life. People expected to live with it, suffer from it and eventually die from it, with only their weekly bottle of medicine for relief. A statistical survey conducted in Sheffield at the time highlighted that bronchitis was twice as prevalent in Attercliffe as in a geographically and socially better appointed area of Walkley. Diphtheria, TB, Nephritis, St Vitus' Dance, measles, rickets and rheumatic diseases in children were all mentioned by Cecil as being very much rarer now than they were then. Against this he commented upon the present day increase in cases of neuroses presented to the medical practitioner. Mental disorders were handled in one of two ways around the time of the second world war. If it was relatively minor you kept it to yourself; people exhibiting symptoms of any severity found themselves occupying one of the couple of thousand beds that were housed in Middlewood, the local psychiatric hospital, which was not a pleasant experience. On reflection, Cecil conceded that with certain exceptions—for example, the comparatively recent use of penicillin for pneumonia and the emergence of the sulphonamide drugs, the first synthetic drugs effective against common bacterial infections—what was actually cured in the way of disease was quite limited.

At a more general level we talked about the similarities between then and now; especially the concern with treatment of diseases rather than their causes. Cecil reflected upon the hopes and aspirations that socialist doctors like himself had held out for the National Health Service and the disappointments they had subsequently experienced when, for example, the post-war Labour government introduced prescription charges and when general practitioners resisted co-operating together in health centres. Above all, he was saddened by the current growth of private practice. Cecil's recollections have proved extremely useful in helping me frame the arguments and ideas which are to occupy the pages that follow.

Kay Habeshaw and Jessie Vaughan   I spoke next to Kay Habeshaw and Jessie Vaughan. Both are now over 70 and have lived in Sheffield all their lives. They related vivid stories of the effect that 'payment for services' had on those who fell outside the insurance scheme, which covered, as Cecil Foggitt had told me, only working men and women and working sons and daughters. The effect touched both the working class families themselves and the general practitioners who provided their services.

Bills from general practitioners were always hard to meet, they told me. Many doctors' bills would never get paid, which led to a number of them accepting the odd 6d, or (ironically) a packet of fags, and usually, as Cecil had also told me, seeking payment at the time of the visit. Kay remembered especially a doctor in the Crookesmoor district of Sheffield who employed a debt collector—'a man in black leggings who came round on Monday mornings'. 'You were always owing the doctor.' The effects were particularly severe for working class women, who due to a policy of not employing married women in Sheffield always tended to fall outside the insurance scheme. 'Mother never had the doctor.' 'You just didn't go to the doctor unless you were on your last legs.' Kay recalled how her own mother hadn't gone to the doctor even though she was in bed with asthma. And Jessie likewise how her mother continued to suffer with high blood pressure, even though she knew that tablets were available which could have helped to lessen her condition. Kay remembered too the severe disapproval that was directed towards one particular woman, who was castigated for 'wasting her husband's money' when she had sought medical care.

It was true that there was Poor Law coverage for people who could prove poverty. But the qualifications were very strict. Jessie remembered one case where somebody had been told to sell a treasured clock before they would be considered eligible. And anyway, they both insisted, the feeling that it was degrading to accept charity and a strong sense of independence kept people from taking up assistance except in the severest situations.

Even for the working people who were covered by insurance, life was not free from the pressures of ill-health. When you were ill, you were 'on the panel'. You were not allowed to go out at night: they thought that the curfew hours were 6 p.m. in the winter and 9 p.m. in the summer. And they recalled how people 'on the panel' would shun even light domestic work for fear of being caught out by one of the 'spies' who were sent out to check up on people who were off work.

Kay's impression, which she backed up with the experiences she recounted, was that the sections of the population who benefited most from the National Health Service were middle aged women and children. She and Jessie confirmed Cecil's recollections on the state of child health. 'Every child had measles, mumps and chicken pox', many were left with sight and hearing impairments for the rest of their lives as a result of the complications that ensued. Jessie recollected how, when she taught at the Langsett Road school, she once had less than half a class at school as the result of measles. Bronchitis was considered 'nothing'. And they commented on the comparative rarity with which one now encounters 'crippled' children. They remembered the rudimentary immunisation programmes that were introduced prior to the NHS, and also the effect that the war-time emergency medical scheme had on pregnant women. 'There were some beautiful babies born during the war.' Kay's summing-up was that the 'NHS had been wonderful for children's health.'

As regards the hospital system, they thought it unlikely that most ordinary people would have been aware of the differences in the quality of care between the voluntary and the municipal hospitals. Kay remembered particularly the barrier to hospital care posed by the 'recommend system', whereby to gain admission to a voluntary hospital you had to have a 'recommend' from the employer of the father of the household.

And with respect to mental illness they confirmed what Cecil had told me. It was considered a 'shameful thing' to have—both for the individual and for the relatives.

They did not believe that the introduction of the National Health Service had been totally without its drawbacks. They spoke particularly of the erosion of the spirit of independence and Kay commented, a little sadly, that it had destroyed a lot of folk medicine. But they were in firm unanimous agreement on where the balance of the advantages and disadvantages fell for ordinary working people.

Horace Windle and Nellie Windle   Lastly I spoke to Nellie and Horace Windle. Both, too, are Sheffield born and bred. They reinforced much of what I had been told of the financial relationship between the general practitioner and the patient. They remembered too the 'sixpenny doctor'—they thought there were a few around Sheffield—and the efforts of the doctor to get bills paid. In the locality that Nellie recalled it was the doctor's wife who acted as debt collector, demanding of working class wives how they would feel if their husbands returned home from work without any wages.

What I particularly gained from talking to Horace and Nellie was a picture of the extent to which the doctor was seen as a last resort. They related a frequent comment that somebody or other 'ought to have the doctor, but look at what they charge'. Before I arrived Nellie had written down a long list of home remedies that ordinary working people would have practised themselves. And she emphasised the role that one particular druggist, whose name was George Owen, had played in administering them and many other forms of primary care.

On Nellie's list were the liquorice powder that the whole family took every Friday night to prevent constipation; the stone jam jar that was kept in the oven containing chopped liquorice, linseed and water, which was stewed for a long time, adding water for consistency, and given to adults and children for coughs; the powdered sulphur that was blown down a rolled sheet of newspaper in the event of a sore throat, which was feared as a prelude to diphtheria; the melted tallow candle in which a brown paper vest was soaked for wear by a child with a sore chest. Five ha'p'orth of oil of almonds, tincture of rhubarb, syrup of figs, tincture of myrrh and syrup of violets was administered as a cure-all for sick children. Quinine was taken by adults for bad colds. Laudanum, bought from an ordinary general grocer, was put on a baby's dummy to quieten it at night. A linseed poultice, made up by pouring boiling water onto linseed until it swelled, left to cool then spread on a calico vest, normally made from an old pillow slip, was worn at the onset of pneumonia.

Nellie recalled how her own daughter had contracted pneumonia as a baby and how she had been administered an antiphlogistic (to draw off the inflammation) which would be stood in a tin in boiling water until it became like chewing gum and then spread like dripping onto a pillow case vest. And also she recalled the prevalence of festering and gathering sores, due she felt to a lack of vitamins in the diet, which would be treated by bread poultices.

Such a system of health care would not, as Nellie and Horace stressed, have been possible without a very supportive neighbourhood. 'There was always somebody prepared to give you an old pillow slip', they recalled. Whether the spirit of community had bred the system of care, of the care bred the spirit of community, it was impossible to judge. But the passing of that spirit was something that they both sadly regretted.

Suddenly, Horace and Nellie remembered the 'amoid man'. He used to hold a stall in the market, drawing a massive crowd and selling a mysterious substance of unknown composition called 'amoid'. People would come with every manner of complaint and leave clutching their tins of 'amoid'.

Nellie recalled how, when she had worked as a part-time secretary at a local school, there had been an epidemic of mumps, which she subsequently contracted. This led to an absence of two weeks, when she received no sickness payment because as a part-time worker she had not been paying insurance stamps.

On maternity care generally, they appreciated the present benefits though they did feel that Nellie had received fairly good ante-natal care, probably because they were both very aware of its importance and ensured that she got it. It was, in fact, the opportunity for ordinary working women to take maternity leave that Horace saw as the greatest benefit over the last 40 years. They both agreed that the National Health Service had a great effect on the general public, particularly the working class, who were now no longer 'afraid to go to doctors'.

And since the National Health Service

It would be wrong to attribute all the advances and improvements that can be recorded solely to the National Health Service. Improved nutrition, immunisation programmes, advances in medical care would probably all have occurred without a National Health Service, and some of the benefits would have filtered down to ordinary working people. The NHS was part of a 'package' of welfare services that have been introduced since the war, particularly by the post-war Labour government. Some commentators, particularly those writing from the United States of America, have argued that the NHS has been of most benefit to the middle classes. They can offer a broad range of statistics on the use that different social classes make of the services to support this argument. The statistics do demonstrate clearly that social class inequalities in health and ill health have persisted, possibly even increased, with the National Health Service. They are alarming. But to concentrate exclusively upon them would be to ignore the very real alleviation of suffering, and particularly worry, that the NHS has brought about for ordinary working people, as recounted in the conversations that I have recorded.

The National Health Service did not have to take on the form that it did. Others were possible and they would have equally met the requirements of the middle classes and the medical profession—the two sections that it is often argued have benefited most from the NHS. Underlying the National Health Service, on paper at least, was a very important principle. This was the principle that the best of existing health care should be equally available to every section of the population. It was this principle that meant most to the ordinary working man or woman.

As we shall see, the principle has often been more of an aspiration than a reality and has not been implemented with the thoroughness that those who fought so hard to build the service upon it would have hoped. Members of different social classes do still have very different *ease of access* to health care, different *quality* of health care available to them and different *experiences of ill-health*. These differences are not random, but operate in a remarkably consistent direction.

And as I was reminded, the service had not also been without its drawbacks. Kay, Jessie, Nellie and Horace all testified to the erosion of the spirit of independence and community that they clearly valued as part of pre-war Britain. Again, it would be wrong to attribute these drawbacks totally to the introduction of the National Health Service. Though it is true that the NHS has delivered health care in a way that does not, to say the least, encourage independence and community but generates reliance upon the medical profession.

Cecil, Kay, Jessie, Nellie and Horace all agreed when I offered them my own assessment of the National Health Service. That is that the principles upon which the service was arguably founded held out a promise, or series of promises, to the ordinary working man or woman, but that these promises have only been realised in a highly piecemeal and diluted form. It might be more accurate to talk about the *potential* of the National Health Service rather than the *principles* of the National Health Service.

In this book I will be examining why this dilution of potential has occurred. The argument will be illustrative rather than exhaustive. Large areas, such as the treatment of psychiatric ill health, the mentally and physically handicapped, the aged, child health, the provision of contraception, abortion and childcare, will only receive passing reference where they justify complete books in their own right.

I will be suggesting that the National Health Service has demonstrated the impossibility of trying to establish islands of socialism in a sea of capitalism. To argue for equal 'health chances' is to argue for a principle which extends beyond asserting that people should have the same access to health care to asserting *also* that people should have the same risks of ill-health. This is a statement about the basic principles of the society within which we live. The argument for *both* the equal availability of health care *and* the equal availability of 'good health' *is* an argument for socialism.

Sections of society have different health and ill-health because they experience the consequences of the way society is organised differently. They have different experiences of employment and unemployment; different patterns of eating, smoking and drinking; different standards of housing; different environments in which to live; different standards of education; different family circumstances. These, and other differences have consequences for people's health and ill-health. I will begin in the following chapter to examine these differences and their health consequences. That is, I will argue that a capitalist organisation of society *produces* illness. I will also show how sections of this society can then turn such illness to their advantage—one could say that these sections *depend upon* people's ill-health.

In the subsequent chapter I will examine the way that the capitalist organisation of society has consistently eaten away at the potential that socialists, in particular, worked hard to incorporate into the National Health Service. I will look at the origins of the NHS, and how the capitalist 'principle of the market' has been allowed to subvert the socialist 'principle of equality'. I will look at the consequence of this in producing the noted mismatch between the need for health care and its availability, and also in the way that successive governments have used the NHS as an economic regulator, turning funds on and off, not in response to social need but in response to economic policy.

In the last but one chapter, I will consider what has to be done if we are to renew the fight for a socialist health service. I will argue that we must work to broaden the scope of the service recognising that the fight for good health for all is not just a fight for good health care *facilities* but also a fight for good health *chances*. This implies that we must also seek an increase in democratic control of the National Health Service—in order that ordinary working people can take their part in moulding it into a form which more adequately suits their needs now.

Lastly, I will speculate upon the form that health and health care might take within a genuinely socialist society. This is difficult, as it is impossible to know with any accuracy. The process of making that society will determine the details. But it is possible to form some idea of the broad characteristics which might be encountered in people's experiences of ill-health and the provision of health care that these experiences will necessitate. This I will do in the final chapter.

2.

Capitalism Makes You Ill

Inequalities in health

During the period of the 1974–79 Labour government, the Secretary of State for Health established a working group to examine 'inequalities in health'. The group had four members: Sir Douglas Black, chief scientist at the Department of Health and Social Security (until April 1978) and president of the Royal College of Physicians; Professor J. N. Morris, professor of community health in the University of London at the London School of Hygiene and Tropical Medicine; Dr Cyril Smith, secretary of the Social Science Research Council; and Professor Peter Townsend, professor of sociology at the University of Essex. The group which was chaired by Sir Douglas Black became known as the Black Working Party, and was particularly well constituted to complete the specific tasks it had been set:

    i. To assemble available information about the differences in health status among the social classes and about factors which might contribute to these, including relevant data from other industrial countries;

    ii. To analyse this material in order to identify possible causal relationships, to examine the hypotheses that have been formulated and the testing of them, and to assess the implications for policy; and

    iii. To suggest what further research should be initiated.

The working party produced its report, which became known as The Black Report, in August 1980. By then the Labour government had been replaced by a right-wing Conservative government led by Margaret Thatcher, to which the report's broad conclusions, that there still persist 'unacceptable' social inequalities in health and that there are a number of social 'improvements' which could be implemented to help eradicate them, were a severe embarrassment.

Normally, a report such as this would have been produced as a properly bound and printed book by the government's publishers, Her Majesty's Stationery Office, and sold to members of the public. The Conservative government made its disapproval of the report's recommendations quietly known, and then, in a half-cocked attempt to avoid their further dissemination, decreed that only 263 cyclostyled copies should be made available, directly obtainable from the DHSS. This number of copies was less than would have been needed to supply every Member of Parliament, for whom reading of such a report should have been mandatory. This bungling piece of suppression ensured the report's notoriety. Photocopies of photocopies circulated academic departments of polytechnics and universities, and meetings were convened by more progressive health authorities in order to discuss its implications. The contents were dynamite enough without the government helping to fuel their explosiveness by its treatment of them.

So what exactly did the Black Report say that the Conservative government found so hard to swallow and that seemed such a damning indictment of Tory ideology? The report was concerned with the health and ill-health experiences of the different social classes. 'Social class' is itself a difficult concept to measure. The Black Working Party was forced to fall back on the most usually employed, but often criticised, definition of social class. This is based upon people's occupations and normally referred to as the 'Registrar General's social classes'—see table 1.

This classification is open to a number of objections. Most serious of which, for our purposes, is that it allows us to find out very little about social differences among women, for as soon as they are married they are assumed to adopt the classification of their husband.

Nor even is 'health' an easy concept. We normally consider it as the absence of observable symptoms associated with a known illness or disease. But, as we will see later, in chapter seven, this is a very restricted understanding.

The Black Report reviewed a broad range of previously conducted studies and was thus forced to adopt the categorisation employed within them. It showed, drawing upon the evidence contained in these studies, that there were frequently recurring 'social class gradients' in the patterns of mortality (what people die from) and the patterns of morbidity (what people suffer from) throughout British society. That is, that for almost every measure of ill-health that the working party examined it found that members of social class V were consistently more likely to suffer from it than members of social class I, with members of the intermediary social classes being ranged progressively between them—see, for example, diagram 1.

Table 1

Social class	Examples of occupations	Percentage of population (1971)
I Professional	Accountant, architect, chemist, church minister, doctor, lawyer, surveyor, university teacher	4.7
II Intermediate (managerial and lower professional)	Aircraft pilot or engineer, chiropodist, farmer, manager, Member of Parliament, nurse, police or fire-brigade officer, schoolteacher	16.2
IIIN Skilled non-manual	Clerical worker, drafter, sales representative, secretary, shop assistant, telephone supervisor, waiter	10.7
IIIM Skilled manual	Bus driver, butcher, bricklayer, carpenter, cook, electrician, miner (underground), railway guard, upholsterer	35.1
IV Partly skilled	Agricultural worker, bartender, bus conductor, fisher, machine sewer, packer, postal worker, telephone operator	15.5
V Unskilled	Kitchen hand, labourer, lorry driver's mate, messenger, office cleaner, railway porter, stevedore, window cleaner	6.9

Source: I. Reid, *Social Class Differences in Britain*, London: Open Books 1977, p. 33, after: *1971 Census of Population*.

The gradient started at birth, was particularly marked in childhood, and persisted throughout life—see diagram 2. Its effect was probably best summarised by Nicky Hart, of the University of Essex, who acted as research fellow to the Black Working Party, when whe wrote:

The risk of premature death is correlated with social class throughout the entire lifetime . . . Expressed in terms of life

It Makes You Sick

Diagram 1
Mortality by social class and cause of death: standardised mortality ratios for
men and married women (by husband's occupation) aged 15–64

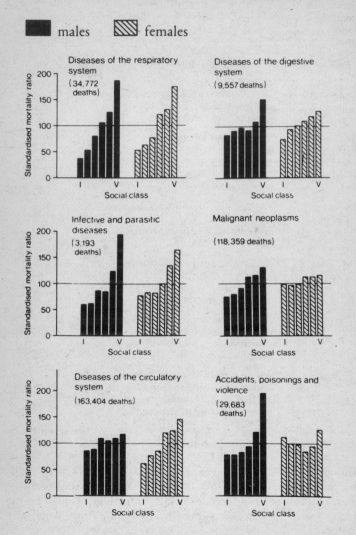

Source: L. Doyal, *The Political Economy of Health*, London: Pluto Press
1979, p. 64, after: *Occupational Mortality 1970–72* London: HMSO 1977.

Note to diagram 1: the measure represented on these bar charts is known as the 'standardised mortality ratio'. Since the age distribution of each social class varies, measures of mortality need to be 'corrected' in case differences in the number of deaths observed are simply reflections of the differing age structures. The standardised mortality ratio is the ratio of the number of deaths found in a particular group divided by the number of deaths that could be expected in that group if the national mortality pattern were to apply, multiplied by 100. Thus, an SMR over 100 means that a group is experiencing more than its fair share of deaths from the condition under consideration.

Diagram 2
Mortality by social class and age

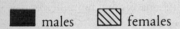

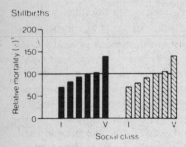
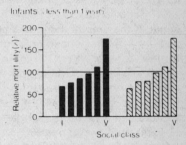

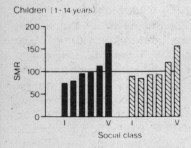
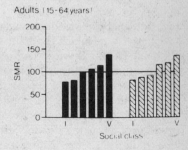

Source: L. Doyal, *The Political Economy of Health*, London: Pluto Press, 1979, p. 63, after: *Occupational Mortality 1970–72*, London: HMSO 1977.

expectancy, this class difference in life chance means that children born to parents in professional occupations, if they themselves are not socially mobile, may expect to spend more than
five years more on earth than the hapless offspring of the un-
skilled.

These gradients can be seen not only when looking at what people
die from (mortality) but also when looking at what people suffer from
during their lives (morbidity). It is, for obvious reasons, easier to
decide when someone is dead than when they are ill. Death is a
recorded event; ill health is only recorded in certain situations, such
as when it leads to a period off work. Morbidity statistics are,
therefore, less reliable and less comprehensive than mortality statistics. Despite this, the Black Working Party was able to assemble
evidence from a variety of ad-hoc studies that similar social class
differences also exist for patterns of illness.

Why should these social class gradients persist? They were known
about at the time of the foundation of the National Health Service,
and it was in the hope of eradicating them that many people argued
for just such a service. One contributory factor is the different access
that social classes have to and the different use they make of the
existing services. The Black Working Party also examined evidence
in these areas. Specifically, it reviewed studies that had investigated
the different ways that social classes use general practitioner services,
hospital care, preventive services and services for the disabled and
infirm. It reported that 'some uncertainty remains as to the existence
of inequalities in the first two cases, there are no grounds for doubt in
the case of preventive services in particular'.

Lack of routinely collected data prevented the working party from
building up a very clear picture. What it tended to find was a fairly
regular social class gradient in the opposite direction—that is, that
social class V members generally make less use of the facilities of the
National Health Service than social class I members, taking into
account their additional experience of ill-health. Members of the
social classes that would appear to need them least know how to get
the best out of available services; but also, these services are located
geographically in such a way as to give them much easier access. This
situation of mismatch was dubbed by Welsh GP J. Tudor Hart, in the
Lancet in 1971, 'the inverse care law': 'The availability of good
medical care tends to vary inversely with the need for it in the
population served.'

But these differences, in ease of accessibility and patterns of usage, could only account for a relatively small proportion of the margin of difference in the health and ill-health experiences of the classes. Improvements in service provision would make a small, though not negligible, impression on this margin. Some of the major contributions to the size of the differences between the classes fall outside the area of service provision. For example, the incidence of death from fire, falls and accidental drowning is 10 times as high in male children in social class V as it is in social class I; cancers of the stomach are more than twice as frequent in men aged 15–64 in social class V as in social class I; even the stomach ulcer (so frequently misrepresented as a 'disease of affluence') is approximately four times as likely to lead to the death of a male aged 15–64 in social class V as to that of his counterpart in social class I.

To make any impression upon these differences it is necessary to change the ways that the social classes varyingly experience the society in which they live. They experience differently the consequences of a social and economic system which is dependent upon the production and consumption of goods, not for the needs that they satisfy, but for the profits they generate.

For a capitalist economy to continue it must be repeatedly generating and accumulating capital. This is its life-blood, the only source of which is profit. Attempts have been made to soften the consequences of this process; the National Health Service can be seen to be one of them. But they cannot change the fundamental dynamic, which must depend upon the existence of a large workforce, which neither receives a due return for the labour it puts in, be it paid employment or unpaid domestic work, nor participates in deciding the use to which the products of its work will be put. The workers are expected to be passive receivers, of jobs, housing, food, environment; and passive receivers of the consequences for their health.

These consequences are confronted daily by women and men in their places of paid employment, their homes, their travel between the two, and even in the relationships and friendships that they form. To reduce the inequalities in health we must look in more detail at these, and ultimately at the structure of the capitalist economy.

Employment

We are reminded starkly of the hazards faced by sections of the population in their employment whenever a major accident hits the headlines of the popular press. The explosion that ripped apart the

Nypro chemical plant at Flixborough near Scunthorpe on Saturday 1 June 1974 killing 28 people, the collapse of the Norwegian Alexander Kielland oil-rig which killed 123 people, are front-page reminders of the extreme hazards faced by parts of the workforce. But until the first serious explosion in a nuclear power station, it is unlikely that such 'major accidents' will add up to more than a fraction of the deaths and injuries that regularly strike people in the course of their occupations, many of which we do not recognise to be especially hazardous.

Health and safety statistics are published annually by the government's Health and Safety Executive. They show that every year six or seven hundred people die in industrial accidents. Mining and quarrying, construction and the transport and communication industries all, not surprisingly, experience more than their fair share of fatalities. A not inconsiderable number of these are preventable. Capitalist ideology would have us believe that accidents occur because workers are careless, when in reality it is the frantic drive to produce capital that is careless with workers' lives. All too many accidents are a consequence of management's efforts to shave costs in search of every possible additional fraction of profit or of workers subjecting themselves to 'unnecessary' risks in pursuit of productivity bonuses.

These minor and major accidents are alarming, but even they pale alongside the effects of *diseases* which are known to be a direct result of people's employment situations. Published statistics could never tell us the full extent of these. Nor would it be right to try to separate them out from the other sources of ill-health that we will be examining later in this chapter. People who take up the most hazardous employment *also* occupy the poorest housing, live in the worst environments, consume the worst diets. For example bronchitis will in many cases be the combined outcome of working in a dusty atmosphere, inhaling polluted inner city air and living in a damp house. The inability to identify a single cause is the let-out for governments who can get away with acknowledging and compensating only a handful of diseases as occupationally related. In order for a disease to be 'prescribed', as it is called, two extreme conditions must be satisfied. It must occur very rarely in the general population; and it must reach near epidemic proportions in the occupational group considered potentially at risk. It was only because the asbestos related diseases, asbestosis and mesothelioma, fulfilled both of these conditions that they have been officially acknowledged as industrially related. Contrast these, again, with bronchitis. This occurs so feequently among the population generally, particularly those sections from which most industrial workers are drawn, that nearly everybody in any particular occupational grouping would have to contract it before that occupation would stand out from the rest of the population with respect to its pattern of bronchitis, as judged by conventional statistical methods. Thus, almost by definition, only rare diseases affecting small numbers of people will be 'prescribed'. The major killers go uncompensated. The frequency with which asbestosis and lung cancer occur together has led the Health and Safety Executive to acknowledge that 'it tends to confirm that asbestos is responsible for a number of cases of lung cancer'. Asbestos workers contracting *only* lung cancer do not receive compensation.

There are limits then to what we can learn about industrially related diseases from official statistics of compensation payments. A more thorough analysis of the relationship between occupation and mortality is conducted by the government once every 10 years. In order to compare patterns of mortality across the occupations, and thus also across social classes which are derived from occupations, it is necessary to 'standardise' mortality rates, as described above, to allow for the differing age structures of these occupations. As explained above, to record that there were more deaths from lung cancer among miners in a particular year than there were among professional footballers in the same year might simply reflect miners as a group being older than footballers and thus more likely to contract lung cancer.

The age-structures of the different populations, which are needed to do the standardisation, are only known once every 10 years, when the Census of Population is conducted. A special monitor of death certificates coincides with the 10-yearly Census of Population. The results are often very slow to be published. Thus, the 1970–72 decennial supplement on *Occupational Mortality*, based on the 1971 census, was not published until 1978, by which time patterns may have changed considerably. However, in the same way that it provided the bulk of the evidence on different mortality patterns between social classes, which we have already reviewed, it also told us much about mortality patterns between different occupations. Miners and quarrymen were two and a half times as likely to die from 'tuberculosis of the respiratory system' of 'bronchitis, emphysema and asthma' as were members of the general public. Furnace, forge, foundry, and rolling mill workers were one and a half times as likely to die from 'malignant neoplasms of trachea, bronchus and lung' (lung cancer) and nearly twice as likely to die from 'bronchitis, emphysema and asthma'. The *Occupational Mortality* supplement shows that large numbers of occupations have their special risks, particularly those that are combined together to form the social classes IIIM, IV and V, but only very few are compensated.

As more detailed studies are being conducted a longer list of chemicals and other substances shown to be directly related to the occurrence of cancers in particular sites or to induce other forms of disease can be drawn up. A directory of toxic substances can be found as an appendix to *The Hazards of Work* by Patrick Kinnersly. But it would be wrong to think of these hazards as being confined to the predominantly male blue collar industrial workforce. The excellent *Office Workers Survival Handbook* produced by the British Society for Social Responsibility in Science has highlighted the hazardous nature of substances and processes handled daily by predominantly female white collar office workers. Correcting fluids, cleaning fluids, electrostencil machines, photocopiers, are all potentially hazardous for people that use them regularly.

Blue and white collar workers also feel the less tangible, but no less real, health effects of 'stress'. This has particularly increased with the extension into the office of work patterns traditionally associated with the industrial workplace. Stress may be caused by the monotony of certain jobs, the working of excessive overtime or the disruption of family and social life that comes from working a shift system. It can lead to an increase in a wide range of complaints and diseases, from headaches to heart trouble.

The effects of stress at work experienced by busworkers in Leeds were the subject of a pioneering investigation carried out by shop stewards of the Transport and General Workers Union 9/12 branch. As well as investigating aspects of busworkers' jobs directly related to the bus, such as cab design and the effects of noise and pollution in heavy traffic, the investigation also considered the impact of buswork and the patterns of life it dictates, on the home and personal life. In measuring the health reaction, they highlighted the important relationship between the work and the domestic situation.

Stress is only one of the hazards of work that is brought into the home. The families of workers in the asbestos industry, the families of woodworkers, have both been recorded as experiencing 'occupational diseases' associated with asbestos dust and sawdust. There are undoubtedly others, though detection proves difficult as the 'methodological' problems identified above, derived from the masking of a

large amount of industrially related ill-health, intensify if we also try
to consider members of the immediate family.

Unemployment

Ironically, it is the sections of the population who are most frequently
exposed to the hazards of employment who are also most frequently
exposed to the hazards of its opposite—unemployment. The effect of
unemployment, or even the threat of it, on workers' blood pressure
and their 'illness behaviour' was the subject of intensive study by a
group of American researchers, S.V. Kasl and his colleagues, in the
late sixties and early seventies—prior to the real depth of the current
economic recession. The increase in short-term, and to a lesser extent
long-term, stress may not perhaps have needed demonstrating,
though the consequences for physical well-being that they uncovered
may have been less obvious.

A separate American research programme has examined the varia-
tion over time of the pattern of mortality from chronic diseases and
its relationship to variations in rates of unemployment. In both the
United States of America and England and Wales, the main worker
on the programme, Harvey Brenner, has reported a series of 'lagged
effects' by which unemployment is argued to yield delayed effects on
mortality at intervals varying by disease. These conclusions are open
to criticism and alternative interpretations. It has, for example, been
argued that the effects are lagging behind peaks of prosperity. But
the vehemence with which the Conservative health minister has tried
to challenge these findings, and the shaky foundation from which he
has launched this challenge, demonstrate the threat which he rightly
believes such findings are to the pursuit of a right-wing monetarist
economic policy.

Housing

The house that someone lives in is perhaps the most immediate
reflection of their economic status. 'Poor' housing can take distinct
forms. Houses suffering from damp, structural defects, overcrowding, lacking a bathroom, an inside WC or other basic amenities,
display obvious, and often measurable, impediments to good health.
Other houses—or more commonly flats—may be in excellent structural condition but provide very inadequate 'homes' for the families
that inhabit them. Living in a town such as Sheffield, with its prolif-

eration of inner city housing estates, you constantly see high rise blocks which would elsewhere be highly sought-after *pied-a-terres* for young married couples, or purpose-built student and young unmarried persons' accommodation. They are currently occupied by families with children who find life there so stressful that the council are having to advertise for people to take them over, when they fall empty, despite waiting lists for council property in other parts of town which have left large numbers of people queueing for years.

The complex nature of 'poor' housing, and the extent to which it occurs simultaneously with other factors of social stress—poor jobs, poor environment, the threat of unemployment, etc.—has made it very difficult to obtain clear evidence of how particular housing deficiencies cause ill-health, though it is very easy to show a general relationship between poor housing and poor health. Numerous studies have shown that in areas where there are measurably poorer housing conditions, there is also higher incidence of physical and mental ill-health.

Shortly before and shortly after the second world war, overcrowding was shown to be significantly related to the incidence of pneumonia and tuberculosis. More recent attempts to identify specific diseases associated with overcrowding have run up against a number of problems. First, the opposite extreme to overcrowding is isolation; and attempts to identify the effects on mental health, in particular, of overcrowding have sometimes ended up demonstrating the more serious effects of isolation. Second, recent re-housing programmes, coupled with the problems already highlighted with some of the more modern council housing estates, do make the picture confused. It is often people who have been living in the most appalling conditions in the past that now, as far as measurable characteristics are concerned, occupy the best housing. The problems of trying to assess the effects of somebody's housing history are immense.

Such 'methodological' problems are not encountered when it comes to assessing the effects of living in dilapidated housing. A large portion of the greater number of deaths from accidents among members of social class V than social class I can be attributed to accidents in the home. The hazards encountered around an old home present particular risks to the very old and the very young, the age groups for which the 'social class gradient' is at its steepest. The same applies to the other two major hazards of dilapidated housing: the consumption of lead from flaking paint, and damp. The very young are much more likely to swallow or to breathe in the lead from poor paint, and the very old are less likely to have the money or the personal capacity to repair old paintwork. The effects of lead can be particularly severe on child development. So too, impairment of lung function, one of the consequences of constant dampness, is a special problem for the growing young and the growing old. The two age groups who, apart from the women and, occasionally, men that they tend to rely on, spend most of their time living in and around the home, are most at risk from its hazards.

The lack of basic amenities within a house—an inside toilet or a bathroom—may not present a direct health risk, but it does contribute to the stresses of occupying poor housing. There stresses will, again, be more severe for those who have others reliant upon them.

The technical problems of assigning specific disease conditions to specific deficiencies in housing standards should not lead us to minimise the direct importance of housing for people's health. The World Health Organisation, in their definition of health, specifically itemise a good standard of housing as one of the characteristics of good health. For them, by definition, anyone experiencing poor housing is experiencing poor health. A number of local authorities now give the district community physician the power to allocate additional points to a tenant's rating on housing waiting lists, on grounds of ill-health. This should be standard practice though it may have little practical value at a time when government economic policy is bringing council house building and repairs to a complete halt. This point was emphasised by Caroline Bedale and Tony Fletcher in the *Times Health Supplement* of 12 February 1982: 'research confirms what people who live in sub-standard housing are in no doubt about—that it is bad for your health—and yet housing has taken the brunt of Government spending cuts.'

Eating, smoking and drinking

It is popular Conservative ideology that what we eat, drink and smoke are purely matters of personal preference and thus, it follows, that if we 'choose' an unhealthy diet or to smoke or to drink too much then we are voluntarily exposing ourselves to risks, which should be viewed in the same ways as the risks they choose to expose themselves to when they voluntarily participate in such pastimes as motor-racing, horse riding or skiing. The other line of the argument is that if we acknowledge, as even Conservative ideology is now forced to do, the prevalence of nutritionally related disease in this country,our only action can be to educate people and exhort them to 'take better care of themselves'—to 'clunk-click' every chip, as it were.

Wider awareness of the importance of diet to health can, of course, be no bad thing. But we also need to ensure wider publicity for the reasons why such unhealthy diets are consumed. In reality, most people, particularly working people, have very little choice over what they eat and, also, less than popular belief would choose to accept, over their patterns of smoking and drinking.

Most food is still bought and prepared by women. Planning, buying, preparing and cooking nutritionally balanced meals is a very time-consuming process. Only the lucky few, which rarely includes working class women, have this time, let alone the necessary in-formation, at their disposal. Buying and cooking meals are 'fitted in'. They are fitted in around a full-time or part-time job, or they are fitted in around the numerous chores of 'keeping house' and raising a family. Still too infrequently these tasks are shared, a woman is just expected to be able to cope.

Not surprisingly, the food that is bought and eaten will be the food that is easy to buy and easy to prepare. It will also be the food that is widely advertised. The food industry is controlled by incredibly few large firms. Bread is the most glaring example. Recent mergers mean that only two companies now enjoy nearly two thirds of the total bread market and over 80 per cent of the standard bread market. The variety of brand names can be deceptive. Large firms will market what is essentially the same product under a host of different names. What these firms produce will not, of course, be what is nutritious but what is most profitable. The foods that are most profitable will be those that can be easily produced and easily marketed. White bread is preferred by manufacturers to brown bread because it suits their more sophisticated machinery and the additives in it give it a longer 'shelf life'. The soft texture and bland flavour, encased in a glossy wrapping, are known to be good for the supermarket shelf, where it pays to be eye-catching and recognisable. Here again, wide advertising is a must. Harassed working class mothers will grab from the shelves what they know and feel they can rely on. They will have no time to peruse labels for ingredients and balanced contents. If something has been seen on the television or hoardings, it will be considered 'safe'.

People will buy what is available. And although 'real bread' shops may be re-opening in the middle class areas of towns, it is still nigh on impossible to find anything other than mass-produced loaves within walking or public transport access of working class estates. Understandably, people will not go to great lengths just to pick up a loaf of bread, or any other basic component of the diet.

And, inevitably, people will buy what they know they can easily prepare. The reason that 'convenience foods' are so widely purchased is because they are precisely that—convenient. A properly balanced meal, made from fresh ingredients, will generally take a longer time to prepare. This is not a particularly inviting prospect, every day, for someone who comes home from a stressful job or someone who has spent a stressful day at home doing domestic labour. Even if you do take the trouble to cook a properly balanced meal it will probably be rejected by children who have been seduced by the sugars and 'tasty' additives of junk food.

What are the consequences of this for the working class diet? The more you earn the more you will tend to eat fruit, vegetables (except potatoes), meat (except tinned meat and sausages), milk and cheese, while the less you earn the more you will eat bread, potatoes and sugar. The poorer sections of society are estimated to get approximately 23 per cent of their energy requirements from bread, compared with the national average of 15 per cent.

These differing patterns of food consumption are reflected in patterns of illness and death. The changed composition of bread has been the major factor responsible for a decrease in the fibre content of diets. This has been directly linked to a number of diseases that are on the rapid increase: appendicitis, diverticular disease of the colon, bowel cancer and ulcerative colitis. Alongside a decrease in dietary fibre, working people consume increased amounts of fats and sugars. These, in their turn, are associated with the incidence of coronary heart disease, in particular. Coronary heart disease is in fact more prevalent among the working classes than among members of the other social classes. Dietary inadequacies are considered to be responsible for a large measure of this difference, compounding the effects that we have already considered of occupying stressful jobs.

These stressful jobs, be they conducted in the home or places of paid employment, take an added toll in another very direct way. They influence patterns of alcohol and tobacco consumption. Overconsumption of alcohol and tobacco should properly be seen as a common symptom of stress rather than wayward habits that people in their foolishness choose to adopt. Most disturbing has been the increase in smoking among working class women at a time when general trends are in the opposite direction. The real scandal of tobacco consumption is the vast sums, and the diverse ways, that the tobacco industry can find to promote its harmful product. Increased public attention, via direct advertising and sponsorship, have more than compensated for any negative effects on demand that may have followed the introduction of the largely unnoticeable 'health warning' or wider publicity for the unhealthy effects of tobacco consumption. The *whole* of the budget of the Health Education Council is merely a fraction of what the tobacco industry spends on advertising. Brian Lloyd, who chairs the Health Education Council, was quoted in the *Times Health Supplement* of 12 March 1982 as estimating that the recently announced sport sponsorship deal would claim 250 lives a year. Sponsorship and advertising put working people particularly at risk. Out of stressed and often isolated lives comes increasing press-ure to find fulfillment in matching up to an externally produced ideal. The media, even without explicit advertising, are all too able and eager to provide the necessary stereotypes. The carefree, happy, good-looking woman or man, with cigarette in hand, is an extremely powerful image against the drab reality of day-to-day existence.

As with most of the other social factors that we are considering it would be wrong to see the health consequences of smoking on their own. Smoking does not only produce the well-publicised disease of lung cancer and the less well-publicised diseases of the heart, it intensifies the risk of contracting many of the other industrially and environmentally related diseases. For example, Sir Richard Doll reported in *Nature* in February 1977, on a number of studies that show that the person smoking over 20 cigarettes a day is more than twice as likely to die from cancer of the pancreas as a non-smoker. One of the studies put this risk at about six times as great.

The alcohol industry has not yet had to find such ingenious mea-sures to compensate for the 'bad press' of government pressure. The freedom of the alcohol industry to advertise and market has been connected with the financial interests of Members of Parliament in that industry. The *Times Health Supplements* of December 1981 listed the family links, industry links and advertising, public relations or other links with alcohol. The list showed that one in 10 MPs has a vested interest in the alcohol industry, with many others having a loose connection.

Food, smoking and alcohol and the industries that produce them have extensive control over people's health. It can fairly be asked whether they are too important to be left in the hands of private enterprise. The unfortunate example of the alcohol industry, particularly its deep penetration into the Tory Party, might raise doubts as to whether parliament can be expected to act any more responsibly.

Transport

Measured in terms of the numbers of years of life expectancy lost, road accidents come second only to lung cancer. Although in absolute numbers road accidents take fewer lives than a number of cancers, unlike these cancers road accidents tend to strike people at an earlier stage in their life. In 1978, road accidents claimed only marginally fewer lives of people under the age of 40 than *all* the cancers added together. Of most concern is that in 1979, not an atypical year, the largest single group of people killed was pedestrians; half as many again as car drivers, nearly twice as many as motorcyclists and over twice as many as car passengers.

The ratio of the risk of death for a child of social class V against that for a child of social class I in a motor vehicle or pedestrian accident is only slightly less steep than the 10 to one ratio that was noted for risk of death from fire, falls and accidental drowning. Comparing standardised mortality rates for social class V against social class I, the respective figures are 245 against 34 for boys and 241 against 54 for girls.

Social class Vs do not own an undue proportion of motor vehicles; they do suffer unduly the consequences of their ownership by others. The picture of social class Is callously knocking down working class kids living on inner-city council estates, as they charge to work from their safe suburban houses, may be an unfair characterisation. But it is an overstatement rather than a misrepresentation.

Much play has been made in advertising in recent years of improved safety standards for occupants of cars. We might have expected some of this attention to be directed to the safety of the pedestrian, if it were the pedestrians that spent money on buying cars rather than the drivers.

The working class might seem less at risk in their greater use of public transport. For every mile travelled as a passenger in a bus or coach you face only one tenth of the risk of being killed that you do if you travel as the occupant of a private car. Also, to quote from an article in the *Times Health Supplement* of 11 December 1981, 'The safety record of British Rail and the London underground can only be described as superb.' Conservative policy of forcing local authorities to put up fares, pushing people from the public sector of transport to the private sector, may in health terms be an uncharacteristic piece of social equalisation. But in reality it is buying the votes of the richer ratepayers with the lives of the working classes.

Air pollution

Road traffic accidents are not the only deadly consequence of private motor transport suffered unfairly by the working class. They also suffer more than their fair share of air pollution.

Motor vehicles give off carbon monoxide and lead. Carbon monoxide, when inhaled, impairs the ability of the blood system to carry oxygen from the lung to tissues and carbon dioxide from tissues to the lung. As a consequence, continued inhaling of polluted air can produce heart disease and damage to the central nervous system. Impairment of the central nervous system by carbon monoxide has led to speculation that carbon monoxide in the atmosphere may be playing a role in the cause of some road traffic accidents.

With respect to lead, there is some dispute as to the major source of lead in the body. Flaking paint has already been identified as one source to which working people in older houses are especially exposed. Food and water both tend to absorb lead which will then be consumed. The lead in water comes from the lead plumbing in older houses and thus may again be a source to which particular sections of the working class are exposed. The bulk of the lead in food, except where there may have been local lead workings, originates from atmospheric lead. It is an ironic thought that a working class holder of an inner city allotment, trying to ensure him or herself the fresh fruit and vegetables mentioned as normally lacking from the working class diet, may in the process be slowly contaminating him or herself with the lead discharged from nearby motor vehicles.

Unlike carbon monoxide, which is a gas, lead is a metal. It is suspended in the air in particles of varying size. Large particles will normally be caught in the nose. Small particles may pass directly through the system. The range of particle size and the levels of exposure that affect an individual will probably vary considerably from person to person, particularly in the case of children, the group most at risk from the lead in the air they breathe.

Consuming lead can affect the digestive system, causing stomach cramps; the blood system, causing anaemia; and the central and peripheral nervous system. It is the last effect that causes most concern with regard to children. There is now substantial evidence that lead levels in large groups of inner city children are so high that their mental, and maybe also physical, development have been seriously retarded. Children with high blood lead levels have been found to suffer from 'hyperactivity'. The effect of lead, particularly on children, was recently examined extensively by a government working party led by Professor P. J. Lawther. Its report *Lead and Health*, also known as the Lawther Report, was published by Her Majesty's Stationery Office in 1980. It was felt by many to be weak with regard to recommendations on levels of lead in petrol, though it pulled together substantial material on the relationship of lead to health.

One combined effect of air pollution and bad diet was identified in investigatory work that was conducted around the Spaghetti Junction in Birmingham—an area where high lead levels have been of special concern. Children were found to be consuming large quantities of lead as they walked down the street eating sticky sweets or lollipops. Lead particles collected on the sticky surface, from which they were licked or swallowed directly.

In certain areas, particularly working class areas, the major polluter of the atmosphere is industry. Industrial processes discharge a vast variety and quantity of substances into the air. Some are gases, others are metals. The installation of more efficient extraction equipment in industrial workplaces is an essential safeguard for the health of the workers employed there. But extraction often merely means dispersing the various substances into the general atmosphere. At worst the health of the workforce inside the factory may only be improved at the expense of those living outside, who may indeed be the very same people.

There is not the space here to list the whole range of substances that are discharged from industrial processes and their individual health effects. The most profuse gas is sulphur dioxide. 'Particulate matter' ranges from the metals, lead, mercury, etc. to asbestos and arsenic.

The geography of the modern industrial city testifies to two centuries of uneven social distribution of the noxious discharges from the production process—and the uneven distribution of the profits that resulted from the process. Such geography is typified by Sheffield. Down-wind and up-hill, the expensive west end housing of Hallam stretches into the magnificent beauty of the Peak National Park. To the east, down-wind, nestled in the industrial heartland of the Don

Valley sits Attercliffe, so polluted by years of industrial waste that the local authority has been forced to make it a housing 'no-go' area.

We no longer suffer from episodes of smog such as those that hit London in December 1952 and again in 1962 teaching us, incidentally and dramatically, the close relationship between air pollution and death. The Clean Air Acts of 1956 and 1968 are a testimony to what can be achieved at a fundamental level for the benefit of the health of working people. They have removed the most visible of the air pollutants, smoke. But the same climatic conditions that produced the build up of smog occur now as regularly as they ever did. And at such times we still experience pollution accumulation. Although they are less visible pollutants, many are equally hazardous to our health. Smoke levels are down dramatically. Sulphur dioxide has shown no such decline. A pair of studies, conducted by members of the Sheffield University community medicine department in 1964 and 1968, on the health of Sheffield schoolchildren showed that at the most seriously affected school in the study, the Carbrook School in Attercliffe, smoke levels dropped from mean daily levels of 301 μg/cm to 169 μg/cm, between these dates, whereas sulphur dioxide levels only fell from 275 μg/cm to 253 μg/cm. Lead and carbon monoxide have increased. From all of these it is still inner city working class housing that suffers most.

Education

If you are looking for an efficient measure to predict the 'health status' of a group of people—that is, the amount of ill-health from which they suffer and die—it can be found in their level of educational attainment. Apart, possibly, from knowing the number of cars that they collectively own, to which it is closely related, knowing the educational achievement, the number of CSEs, O-levels, A-levels etc. of that group would allow you to make more accurate predictions about their health than any other characteristic.

This close relationship is not, of course, for the main part directly causal. Achieving an O-level in mathematics will not produce an immunity against contracting the fibroses that are caused by exposure to asbestos, or other such fibrous matter. But it will lessen the liklihood of having to take up employment in an area within which such exposure occurs.

Education, even more than health, is the prime witness to the persistence of class divisions within the modern capitalist society.

Educational qualification, towards which sections of society still enjoy a privileged headstart, is the key to the attainment of well-paid and prestigious jobs. These, in their turn, bring access to the better housing, better environment and freedom from direct contact with the industrial process, which lead to more chances of a longer, accident-free and disease-free life.

There is, however, a lesser sense in which educational achievement may be said to be directly causal of better health. The class nature of education is reflected in the preparation that the different sections of society are given for the employment positions they are expected to fill. 'Factory fodder' needs to learn the discipline of work. Mechanical repetition of tables and spelling in working class schools is more prevalent than progressive educationalists would have us acknowledge. Social awareness is considered (maybe rightly) positively subversive. On the other hand, potential doctors and children destined for professions rather than jobs will learn the rudiments of human biology and social history. Middle class children are far more likely to know of slums, cholera, social programmes to clean the water and the streets than their working class counterparts to whom this history rightly belongs. The broader education also brings an increased awareness of the hazards of a modern industrial society, an awareness of the need, say, for a properly balanced diet and how it might be obtained. There are class differences too in the nature of leisure-time pursuits, as well as in awareness of the harmful consequences of certain patterns of consumption.

Education cannot *guarantee* a stress-free working, domestic and social life. A necessary component of the dynamic of this society is the competitive aggression which oils the 'wheels of power'. But those who have benefited from a middle or upper class education may more accurately be said to have 'chosen' a particular life-style, together with the health hazards it might present, of which they are more likely to be conscious.

Ethnic minorities

We have, so far, been concerned with the differences that exist between the social classes. Western capitalist society is divided in other ways which overlay or compound social class divisions. It is divided by race and by sex.

Members of ethnic minorities suffer doubly. They are, by virtue of their economic circumstance, as well as the implicit and explicit racism of society, more likely to occupy the jobs and the houses, and to live in the environments, with the problems already described. They will also suffer problems of cultural displacement, with administrators of the health services being unwilling, or slow, to respond to their special needs.

One example stems from the prevalence of vitamin D deficiency among members of the Asian community. This deficiency is the product of a combination of the Asian style of dress, which inhibits exposure to the sunlight, and the Asian diet, which tends to exclude certain foods such as liver, eggs, oily fish and margarine, which are the major sources of vitamin D in the body. The consequence of a deficiency in vitamin D is an increased incidence of rickets and osteomalacia, which are skeletal disorders which can at their severest produce an inability to walk. A solution to this problem which has been proposed by health workers from within the ethnic minorities, such as the Community Health Group for Ethnic Minorities, would be to enrich chapatti flour with vitamin D, as is already done with margarine. The government has rejected this course of action and opted instead for an 'educational programme', exhorting Asians to discard their 'wayward' life styles and adopt a western diet.

It should be stressed that demands made by members of ethnic minorities on the health services are currently very low. This is in marked contrast to the support that they give by occupying the low prestige, low pay, jobs which could otherwise remain unfilled. The age structure of ethnic minority communities is such that they have a very small proportion of elderly people, and their family structure is more supportive of the ill. What special needs they do have deserve to be given serious attention.

Women

The other section of society with special needs, if it is right to call them that, is not a minority but a majority. We have already seen, in a number of ways, how women also suffer doubly. We have also seen how, through the way statistics are collected, women's health problems are 'hidden from history'. The mental stress resulting from this double burden was the subject of a recent study of women in three food factories. Anna Coote, in the November/December 1981 edition of *New Socialist*, quoted from the study at length. The quote is worth repeating here:

These women are caught up in a constant and unremitting round of activity throughout their waking hours. Their day begins early, about 5 or 6 a.m. and finishes late, about 9 or 10 p.m. with little or no time for rest or relaxation, leaving them continuously tired and often emotionally exhausted. Many are responsible for the household budget and under financial pressure to make ends meet, which is a major factor in their going out to work.

But employment has to be fitted in with household duties and childcare arrangements, which they and their families regard as unquestionably their responsibility. Factory work is often seen as the only job possible in the circumstances and entered into more from necessity than choice. although outside employment of some kind was in almost all cases considered desirable.

Women's reproductive role makes them particularly vulnerable to occupational health hazards. A reflection of the attitudes demonstrated in the quote above is that they find themselves occupying the lowest paid, which are also the most hazardous, jobs. They face nearly all the health hazards faced by men and others which are specific to their reproductive system. In many cases they are also facing hazards on behalf of their children who are yet to be born. No recognition is made of the menstrual cycle other than branding women as inferior workers and thus the most dispensable in times of economic contraction. The stress of the constant threat of unemployment is not just something faced by male workers in times of recession. Large numbers of women live with it as a way of life.

The woman that escapes the factory floor and finds her 'proper place' in a clerical job will not be freeing herself from hazards, as the *Office Workers Survival Handbook*, already referred to, amply shows. Nor is there a refuge to be found in the home and in childcare. The complex inter-relationship between domestic labour, childcare and paid employment on the one hand and schizophrenia and depression on the other, among women of different classes, has been the subject of a number of studies by George W. Brown and his co-researchers. Domestic labour is rarely fulfilling and it too can be extremely hazardous. Childcare could be fulfilling, but rarely is. Men must take a large share of the blame for this. Their attitudes towards women and the family are a reflection of an image of themselves and of women. This image arises from the deeply embedded sexism in our society, which is reinforced, sometimes crudely, sometimes subtly, by the media, in their explicit advertising and their contribution to the persuasion that currently defined sex roles are fixed and unchangeable.

Summary

We have ranged over a number of areas in this chapter where the economic and social relations of a capitalist society have a direct influence upon people's health and ill-health experiences. We have only scanned each one briefly. Most could be the subject of books in their own right. Some have been. (These can be found in the bibliography that appears at the end of this book.) There is always the danger of losing the wood for the trees, if each area is probed minutely. The impression that should, however, stand out from this mass of evidence is that there is no way we can address ourselves to the social inequalities in health unless we also address ourselves to the deep-rooted structural causes.

We will return to the implication of some of these ideas when we consider in a later chapter a socialist programme for health and for the National Health Service. The interim conclusion, which is important in its own right, is that we must be prepared to broaden the argument about what rightly constitutes health policy and health planning. When we are discussing employment policy, transport policy, housing policy, we are discussing, very directly, health policy. When the Tories are planning to put another million or so people out of work, they are planning illness. Creating health policy is not an incidental item which can be looked after at some time in the future, as and when we can afford it. What is more, when we are creating strategies for the future, unless we make explicit recognition of the health dimension, we will continue to fall into the same old trap of ignoring the real well-being of people until it is too late.

3.

Profit Comes from Illness

If you were asked to list the characteristics of a civilised society it is unlikely that you would get very far down your list before you wrote down something along the lines that 'no person should be able to benefit from the misfortunes of others'. The ability to profit from the ill-health of others opens the way for every manner of corruption and exploitation, as motives other than a patient's best interest take over. This is not to accuse the people who do very well out of the provision of health services, outside or on the fringe of the public sector, of seeking callously to exploit the suffering of others for their own advantage. Neither, though, is it to go to the opposite extreme—as we more commonly encounter—of praising them and granting public recognition for their good works and altruistic motives.

There is no way we can hope to provide an equitable service for all when health care delivery is open to distortion by outside motivations, however inconspicuous or blatant they might be. In this chapter we will examine three areas: private practice, the drugs industry and the medical technology industry; each of which, over the last 35 years, has made vast profits at the expense of the National Health Service.

Private medicine

It was the socialist goal of the National Health Service that it should provide services which would be free of charge at the time of use. It would seem a little contradictory, given that the NHS was inaugurated by the most radical government this country has probably ever known, that private practice should have been allowed to coexist with the NHS. Rightly or wrongly, Aneurin Bevan, who was the individual with chief responsibility for the final format of the NHS, saw the greatest potential threat to its successful operation lying in the power of the medical profession to subvert it. It is said that he ensured the profession's acceptance of the service by 'choking their mouths with gold'. The prime mechanism through which Bevan created the necessary gold was by allowing them to continue operating private practice alongside, and in close conjunction with, the provision of services to the NHS.

It was always possible that private practice could have been no more than a short term expedient. With the right commitment to the public sector it could have been gradually phased out, as promised in the Labour Party's programme when it returned to power in 1974. We will examine how deep this commitment to the National Health Service has gone in the next chapter. But lack of commitment is not any longer the most serious problem. This is now the very size to which private practice has grown. In recent years it has mushroomed. This growth has been made possible by a systematic under-financing of the NHS, which we will also be examining in the next chapter. It has been accelerated by the ability of private insurance companies to seize the opening for a quick killing and by their ability to exploit the charitable status of private hospitals and nursing homes.

Private health insurance must be the most rapidly expanding industry (arguably the *only* expanding industry) in Britain today. The *Times Health Supplement*, a short-lived weekly newspaper covering health and the health services, carried each week stories of new private facilities opening alongside stories of old decaying public facilities closing (and not being replaced). The Tories are now openly boasting of how they are selling off old NHS hospitals to the private sector. David Widgery, in *Health in Danger*, quotes Jack Massey, who resigned from the chair of Kentucky Fried Chicken to head the Hospital Corporation of America, a Cayman Islands registered company based in Nashville, Tennessee, as saying: 'The growth potential in hospitals is unlimited: it's even better than Kentucky Fried Chicken'.

The accuracy of this prediction is to be found in the experience of the British private insurance companies. From an original total of less than 50,000, at the time that the NHS began, the number of subscribers to the British United Providence Association (BUPA) and the Private Patients Plan (PPP), the two largest insurers, has grown to over one and a quarter million. Their subscription income now exceeds £125 million yielding profits of around £40 million, a very 'healthy' profit rate of over 30 per cent.

Not unnaturally American capital has viewed this sort of profit with astounded and avaricious eyes. It is sweeping into the British private health sector vehemently resolved to carry some of these amazing returns back off across the Atlantic. The American Medical International, based in Los Angeles, owns four hospitals in and around London. Its flamboyant revelling in publicity gimmicks has been well documented in the Politics of Health Group and Fightback's comprehensive pamphlet *Going Private*. Less favourable publicity has been directed against the Hospital Corporation International (UK) Limited, a Sheffield-based offshoot of the Hospital Corporation of America. Their proposal to build a 100-bed private hospital just across the road from the new Southampton General Hospital was perceived by the local public as a blatant attempt to poach the potentially profit-making areas of health care.

The acceptability of resorting to the private sector in the face of, and rather than fighting against, the decline of the public sector has now penetrated deeply into the labour movement. To borrow the quote of a worker in *Going Private*: 'Private medicine is no longer only available to the "rich bastards" '. As part of a wage deal the EETPU negotiated entry into a private medical scheme for 40,000 electricians; 1,000 members of the National Union of Seamen working on oil rigs have their insurance paid by their employers. The British sector of the private insurance market is underpinned by and generating some of its handsome profits for the unions' own insurance funds.

Does all this matter? Is it not possible to agree with Tory ideology that the existence of a private sector 'frees up' resources for the National Health Service, allowing funding to be concentrated where 'it's really needed'—and if people make a quick buck on the side, so what?

It matters a great deal. The existence and expansion of a private medical sector not only feeds off the decline in the NHS, it helps to fuel it.

The reason that people will give for 'going private' is that it offers more comfort, more privacy, and that it allows you to avoid long queues—particularly for minor operations, but also for routine services such as chiropody. Faced with the need for, say, a hip replacement, it is fully understandable that someone should resort to the private sector rather than endure months of extreme discomfort. There clearly *is* an opportunity for unscrupulous medical practitioners to maintain unnecessarily long waiting lists in the NHS in order to encourage patients to see them privately, but the argument for a fully public health service does not rest on the immorality, or otherwise, of doctors. Medical practitioners operating private practice within public hospitals use publicly funded resources for the generation of their own profit. Nursing staff are expected to oversee operations on private patients at the end of an NHS list for no more reward than the occasional box of chocolates. Laboratory staff are expected to 'drop everything' when a private specimen is brought in for analysis.

Could this drain on the public sector be avoided by separating off private practice completely from the National Health Service—simply by abolishing paybeds within NHS institutions? Again the answer is no. Private practice concentrates on the more dramatic and prestigious areas of medical care. These are areas where surgeons can command high fees for comparatively routine operations. Private hospitals can, as a consequence, offer nursing staff rates far in excess of NHS rates (though ancillary and domestic staff will normally receive less). Jeannette Mitchell, reporting on staff shortages in London hospitals in the *Times Health Supplement* of 12 February 1982, wrote that 'nurses can find other work, especially in private hospitals, which pay on average £1,500 a year more and do not have trouble finding staff.' Much sought after nursing staff will be pulled away from those areas where their services are most needed—the care of the aged, the care of the mentally and physically handicapped—the 'cinderella areas' which don't feature in the private insurance companies' prospectuses. There is already considerable concern at the imbalance in the pattern of the provision of health care. Proportionately, if not in absolute terms, too much is spent on the high-technology, acute areas of medicine such as heart transplants and too little on the labour intensive, caring end of the spectrum, such as looking after elderly people. We will look at the reasons for this in the next chapter. Growth of the private sector will intensify this imbalance, starving the caring services even more. Private health insurance holders are the healthy middle aged and the more articulate. The more people opt out of the NHS, the more resistance will grow to adequate funding of a service which offers few benefits to the insured—in the short term, at least. We can only anticipate the re-emergence of a two-tier hospital system of the sort that predated the NHS.

The growth of a private sector can also be detrimental to the direction that health care takes. In terms of the quality and length of people's lives the real successes in health over the last two centuries have been in the arena of 'public health', that is, improved sanitation, disposal of sewage, clean air acts, etc. A revitalised public health movement would turn its attention to how a capitalist society produces ill-health, as we have outlined in the previous chapter. Major improvements in health in the future can only be expected to come from major social changes in these areas. Examples of these will be spelled out in a later chapter. But the move towards high-technology acute sectors of medical care induced by private practice will pull away public attention and public financing from these areas.

If we need more concrete evidence of the consequences of a private health system we should look no further than the United States of America, from where so much of the impetus towards privatisation is coming. Their system is administratively expensive, bureaucratic and maintains good health care as a privilege for the better off. The poor are forced back, at the best, onto charity, at worst, onto nothing; all too closely resembling the picture of health care in Britain before the NHS that we glimpsed in the introduction of this book.

The drugs industry

Recent trade union campaigns have drawn public attention to the growing threat to the National Health Service of private practice. In contrast, the drugs industry has gone largely unchecked, being a complex and multinational enterprise.

Drug multinationals are accountable to no-one. The Swiss giant Hoffman La Roche is protected, by Swiss law, from having to declare the details of its finances to anybody other than its shareholders. One former Roche employee, Stanley Adams, was imprisoned in Switzerland for industrial espionage, and subsequently refused British citizenship, for revealing the company's practice of 'price fixing', though this practice directly contravened Common Market laws on 'free competition'.

Some idea of the profits that the drug multinationals amass can be gained from the following figures. The Roche company's annual turnover is in excess of $1,200 million, 70 per cent of which is accounted for by pharmaceuticals.

Returns after taxes for the drug industry have been estimated to be far in advance of any other industry at 21.4 per cent. (Industrial chemicals came a poor second at 16.2 per cent.) On any estimate Roche's drug profits exceed $200 million a year.

Profits for British firms are no easier to determine than those for the multinationals. The four major British drug firms, Glaxo, Wellcome, Beecham and, particularly, ICI, all engage in other activities than drug production. Profit levels for their drug side are not declared separately. But returns on capital for all their activities are variously declared at between 30 and 50 per cent.

One thing is certain. Drug manufacture is highly lucrative—for those that are in on the market. But how are such enormous profit levels so consistently maintained? The answer is that they are guaranteed by a combination of practices: monopolisation; patenting; marketing the same product under varied names; over-pricing; and advertisement saturation.

Monopolies   Industries will naturally, under capitalism, tend to concentrate, forming larger and larger units which individually, and collectively, control greater proportions of the market. Their domination makes penetration into the market by new, small, enterprises increasingly impossible. Nowhere is this negation of the 'freedom' of the so-called free market more vividly demonstrated than in the drug industry.

The Haslemere Group, in its pamphlet *Who Needs the Drug Companies?* writes:

> Smaller companies were gradually swallowed up or beaten out of the market. In Britain now, five companies control approximately 30 per cent of the market, in the United States, 10 firms control over 40 per cent; the three Swiss firms, Roche, Sandoz and Ciba-Geigy between them account for some 15 per cent of world sales.

One factor creating this monopolisation is the high cost of research and development. No individual, without the underwriting of a large organisation, could possibly embark upon a programme of testing, production and marketing. But equally important is the protection given to the monopolies by the patent laws.

Patent laws   The patent laws guarantee the inventor of a new product sole production rights for a period of 16 years. In 1965, the Labour government established a committee under Lord Sainsbury to investigate the drugs industry. Its report, the Report of the Committee of Enquiry into the Relationship of the Pharmaceutical Industry with the National Health Service 1965–67, considered this period to be too long. Despite this, the Banks Committee, which was subsequently set up to look into the workings of the patent laws generally, recommended the extension of the patent period by a further four years.

The justification for the patenting laws is that they guarantee individual inventors rewards for their ingenuity. Virtually all drugs patents are owned by the multinationals, and are used by them as a mechanism of market control—a screen behind which they can set whatever price they like without fear of being undercut by a competitor.

If a small company does produce a potentially profitable new drug it will be immediately swallowed up by a large multinational, which will thereby acquire the sole right to market it at its own price.

A consequence of the system of patents is that the same drug will be sold under different brand names by the same firm or group to create pseudo-competition (see table 2); and other drugs, with only slightly varying ingredients, will be sold by other firms, in order to circumvent the patent laws.

Brand names There is a bewildering catalogue of named traded drugs. The confusion is compounded by the fact that most drugs have three names, a generic or chemical name, an approved name and a brand name. An exposé of the Thalidomide scandal listed 37 different names under which Thalidomide, either on its own or in combination with other drugs, was marketed—of these 10 were produced by Chemie Grunenthal, who held the patent, and six by the Distillers Company of Great Britain, under licence for Grunenthal. Brand names are employed to create a 'brand loyalty'. They are easier to remember than the complicated chemical names. But they mask the existence of psuedo-competition and they make it much harder for the medical practitioner to know exactly what he or she is prescribing.

John Robson, in the Marxists in Medicine pamphlet *Take a Pill* . . . cited the graphic illustration of Professor Garb, an American professor of pharmacology, who asked what would happen if the drug companies were to take over the manufacture and marketing of beans:

> They would all stop using the word 'beans' and each would give the product a new name. Some might use anagrams like 'Sneabs' or 'Nabes' and others might call them 'LoCals' or 'HiPros'. Picture the confusion in the grocer's store if beans were no longer called beans.

Overpricing The monopoly position of the pharmaceutical multinationals, guaranteed by the patent laws, allows these companies to name their own price. This they do.

Table 2

Examples of pseudo-competition between companies that have a mutual marketing arrangement

The prices of the competing products usually differ little if at all:

cotrimoxazole	Septrim (BW)	Bactrim (Roche)
gentamicin	Genticin (Nicholas)	Cidomycin (Roussel)
cephalexin	Ceporex (Glaxo)	Keflex (Lilly)
tetracycline	Achromycin (Lederle)*	Tetracyn (Pfizer)*
metoprolol	Betaloc (Astra)	Lopresor (Geigy)
sotalol	Sotacor (Bristol)	Beta-Cardone (Duncan Flockhart)
prazosin	Sinetens (Carlo Erba)	Hypovase (Pfizer)
gliptzide	Minodiab (Carlo Erba)	Glibenese (Pfizer)
glibenclamide	Daonil (Hoechst)	Euglucon (Roussel)
ketoprofen	Alrheumat (Bayer)	Orudis (M & B)

*These were the original two brands—generic preparations and other brands now available cost less.

Source: *Drug and Therapeutics Bulletin*, vol. 14 no. 14, 2 July 1976.

Montague Phillips, the co-discoverer of one of the first anti biotics effective against pneumonia wrote in *The People* of 'a scandal that has remained cloaked in secrecy and respectability for more years than I care to remember'. He listed the costs and profits of some of the most commonly used drugs in the NHS and concluded that 'according to my figures, the lowest profit is 320 per cent and highest 5000 per cent.' Librium was sold by Roche to the NHS at £10 per 1,000, though its basic costs came to a mere 4s (20p). These giant profits were often made after competition had originally been eliminated by very *low* pricing. Valium had even been given free to the NHS at first.

If things look bad in the UK, it's worth sparing a thought for the Third World. At the time that the price for tetracycline was $28 per kilogram in Europe, it was $113 in India. When a US congressional study examined comparative prices, it found that prices in India were generally 357 per cent higher than the average European price.

Advertising and promotion   If all this were not enough to ensure drug production as the most profitable industry throughout the world, the drug multinationals go on to exploit the captive nature, dependence for information and altruistic motives of the people who determine the levels of drug usage. This is not, in the main, the patients themselves, but their doctors, particularly their general practitioners. General practitioners are submerged by all kinds of advertising and promotion material.

The Haslemere Group asserts that:

> The general practitioner in Great Britain receives in an average month one hundredweight of advertising literature and assorted free gifts including diaries, notepads and records, from which drug brand names beam out insistently. In addition, s/he will receive frequent visits from drug company representatives, of which there is one for every eight GPs in Britain; will be exposed to advertisements in the free medical newspapers and subscription journals; will be invited to films, drinks, and conferences at home and abroad, all at drug companies' 'expense'; and will receive free samples of drugs given away at an annual cost to the industry of £2 million.

Post-graduate medical education is now virtually dependent upon drug company sponsorship.

Drug safety The claim made by the drugs industry is that the high level of profits is justified because of the cost and risk involved in the research and development process. There may indeed by some truth in this claim. It certainly takes some ingenuity to create new 'needs' in an area which is already supersaturated with the existing, artificial and spurious 'needs'. The drug companies' research is concentrated in the areas of high sales (big profits) at the expense of less common conditions. 'Molecular manipulation', which is the process by which new drugs are created out of existing ones by making small changes to their composition, will be pursued rather than more basic research and rather than investigating and improving the safety of new and established drugs. It is only when there is a tragedy on the scale of Thalidomide that the companies are called to account. The problems of proving the more minor side effects of routinely prescribed drugs are very similar to the problems of proving the ill-health consequences of the industrial process that were discussed in the last chapter. The difference is that the drug companies are making vast profits out of a product which is known to have physiological effects.

The medical supply industry

It may be difficult to estimate levels and rates of profit for the drug companies; but it is completely impossible for the public to know how much the medical supply industry is making from the National

Health Service. The NHS is the largest individual spender of money in the country, outside the Ministry of Defence. It makes occasional very large 'one-off' purchases, for hospitals or major pieces of medical equipment. It also makes very regular smaller purchases, for food, bed linen, medical instruments, etc. A large amount of this money goes as profit to private companies. How can the individual member of the public know whether these profits are 'reasonable' or whether the National Health Service, and that means us, is being 'ripped-off'?

Public attention has recently been drawn to the merits or otherwise of the scanner. Out of the first brain scanners introduced in the early 1970s there have been developed a whole range of whole body scanners, employing techniques of computerised tomography (CT), which processes an array of X-ray images, producing a three-dimensional picture. CT scanners are very expensive. They cost approximately £500,000 to buy, and then up to £100,000 a year to staff and to keep in working order. Additionally, they need to be housed somewhere.

The emotional appeal of scanners is very high. They have replaced renal dialysis units as the favourite gift by charities and other fund-raising organisations. The slogan has been widely brandished that 'scanners save lives'. Whether this is true is very doubtful. Scanners are aids to diagnosis and could never directly assist in 'saving lives'. Maggie Hartford, in the *Times Health Supplement* of 20 November 1981, wrote:

> The only absolute cast-iron evidence of the body scanner's influence in saving lives seems to be the unfortunate case of 56-year-old James Orange. He died on a solo 150-mile sponsored walk to raise money for a £1 million appeal for a body scanner at Newcastle Hospital.

The public are under strong pressure, both from the medical profession and from the medical supply industry, to believe that money spent on sophisticated and technologically advanced 'gadgetry' must be well spent. The scientific officer at the North West Thames Region, writing in the same edition of the *Times Health Supplement*, commented that 'many doctors feel that they must put in a request for something to satisfy their virility'. A specialty which is constantly seeking and spending money will be seen as progressive and go-ahead—thus also doing important things. A specialty which doesn't spend will be seen as stagnant; and dispensable. Technological hardware has more appeal than staff. The secretary of the Leeds Community Health Council observed: 'At the same time as the scanner was accepted the area nursing officer also asked for something like £300,000 to bring nursing staff levels up to national standards—but she just got a committee to look into the question.' It is in consultants' interests to encourage the purchase of the newest equipment. They will be ably assisted by the companies that supply it.

At the height of its domination of the scanner market EMI's sales rose from £321,000 in 1973 to £5 million in 1974 and reached a peak of £93 millin in 1977. Its profits in 1977 were nearly £15 million, though this turned to a sudden loss of £13 million in 1978. EMI's turnabout in fortune came as a result of problems in its research programme at a time when other companies were moving in on the area and when the North American market in particular had been swamped. Some towns in the USA had up to five scanners and many are now sitting idle.

This is not, however, stopping the supply industry from developing newer and more sophisticated versions, nor stopping other multinationals trying to get in on the act. Martin White, European director of the market research company, Creative Strategies International, predicted in the *Times Health Supplement* of 29 January 1982 that 'in the next decade high technology equipment in hospitals, dental surgeries and the home will expand dramatically'. In 1980 European health administrators were estimated to have spent over £2,000 million on medical equipment.

Until recently three companies, Philips, Siemens and General Electric, dominated the medical supply market, 75 per cent of which was supplied from western Europe. Recently, an interest has been developed by Hoffman La Roche and its subsidiaries. As the world's largest pharmaceutical company, enjoying the sort of profit rate that was commented upon above, Roche must find the medical equipment market very attractive in order to risk diversifying in that direction. It would be wrong though to suspect that this somehow implies that the industry is opening up, thereby creating a genuinely free market from which the NHS might gain some benefit. The impossibility of this was also spelt out by Martin White: 'It seems unlikely that a new company that cannot buy its way in will make any inroads into the market . . . The medical electronics industry is increasingly being dominated by large multinationals.'

The medical supply industry has a large bag of tricks at its disposal to ensure the promotion of its products. It is firmly believed that the first anonymous donation of £100,000 that came in for the scanner appeal in Leeds came from EMI: a better strategy than dropping the price of your product. Equipment is loaned to hospitals for 'evaluation' in order to set the 'me-too' principle in motion. Consultants in the same specialties elsewhere and hospitals in surrounding areas will argue that they too must have the same, in order to provide the 'best available' medical care.

Members of the public would certainly share that aim. But it is arguable whether an increased emphasis on medical technology is the best way of achieving it. If we were to scrap plans to buy Trident nuclear missiles we could all have access to our own personal scanner. If only one of them can save a single life or alleviate somebody's suffering, the investment in the rest may have been worthwhile. But unfortunately the price you pay for a luxury is far more expensive in a time of recession. Money spent on medical technology is money that is not available for the less dramatic caring services. Again, we can see the same pull towards the acute sectors of medical care that was noted to be a consequence of the growth of private medicine.

The National Health Service is supplied by private industry with a vast range of items and goods. A scandal which is beginning to be uncovered is the quality of hospital building carried out during the short spurt of hospital construction that took place in, and following, the 1960s. The Royal Hallamshire Hospital in Sheffield was opened as recently as 1978. It has already been dubbed 'Fawlty Towers' by staff working there, whose unions are demanding a public inquiry. It has suffered serious problems of cross infection and accelerating costs of heating and maintenance, from a variety of technical problems centring on its laundry, air-conditioning and lift systems. Even the leader of Sheffield Area Health Authority described it as an 'over-ambitious engineering project which cannot deliver the goods'.

The Royal Hallamshire is not an isolated example. The *Times Health Supplement* of 26 March 1982 reported the evidence of Sir Kenneth Stone, DHSS permanent secretary, to the Commons Committee on Public Accounts in which he stated that £30 million worth of faults have already shown up in buildings put up for the NHS over the past 10 years.

A final illustration of the relationship between private industry and the National Health Service was unwittingly provided by the Conservative government with their decision to sell off the firm of Amersham International at well below its true market price. The resulting prices boom is expected to cost the NHS dearly. The company is the sole UK manufacturer of radioisotopes, widely used in the diagnosis and treatment of disease. Terry Davis MP, Labour's deputy health spokesperson, was quoted in the *Times Health Supplement* of 5 March 1982 as saying:

> Previously, profits made by Amersham out of sales to the NHS went into the Treasury and were available for the government to use for public expenditure, according to their priorities. But now there is no control over the prices charged to the NHS or over their profits from these sales.

Summary

This chapter has examined three areas where private capital is doing very well out of people's ill-health: private medicine, the drugs industry and the medical supply industry. At a time when general economic recession is striking particularly hard into the services provided by the NHS, those on the periphery seem to be passing by relatively unscathed, and in the case of private medicine growing very fat off the pickings.

The point has been stressed that the effect of this parasitic relationship is not just to starve the National Health Service of funds, to make money less available generally for all types of health care, it has been also to distort the pattern of health care delivered under the NHS. In the next chapter we will examine both these areas in more detail: the funding of the National Health Service and the pattern of health care available under it.

4.

A National Health Service Under Capitalism?

The drugs industry, the medical supply industry and private practice are areas where the socialist potential of the National Health Service is being systematically and consistently undermined. In theory, a future Labour government, with sufficient radical will, not just a radical programme, could go a long way towards halting this erosion at the base. The first two could be nationalised (though this would still not tackle the problems of the vast multinational involvement in these areas, nor, immediately, correct the distortion to the pattern of health care) and private practice could be abolished, by a combination of measures. These would be important steps. They would go a long way, practically and ideologically, towards reclaiming the NHS for the benefit of the people of this country.

The most important determinant of the shape of the NHS in the future is political will—the political will of the government as it reflects and shapes the political will of the people. The political will of the Conservative Party is, and has been throughout the life of the NHS, fairly obvious.

The political will of the emerging Social Democratic/Liberal Alliance is very unclear. They are certainly not planning any major redirection of the National Health Service, which would only run them up against business and class interests that they are frantically trying to court. The political will of the Labour Party has been ambivalent, with lots of rhetoric and promises when in opposition, but very little in the way of real socialism when in power. This has been epitomised by its wavering attitude towards nationalisation of the drugs industry and abolition of private practice.

In practice, it seems to have made very little difference over the last 35 years which colour of government has administered the National Health Service. We will see, in the first half of this chapter, how both Labour and Conservative governments have used the NHS as a means of regulating the economy; turning funds off and on, not in response to any objective measure of need, but as it suited their economic strategy. Neither has developed a strategy for the health service, in its own right. We will see, in the second half of this chapter, what the consequences of this have been for the NHS. We will see how it has become a national sickness service, or a national repair service, mopping up those few of the casualties of the capitalist economy that it can.

The National Health Service as a regulator of the capitalist economy

1945–51: Uncertain beginnings These comments might seem extremely unfair on the post-war Labour government. Returned to power after the war, there is little doubt that it set about reshaping Britain, as it had promised it would, with a will and with a commitment to a radically restructured social and economic base. The very existence of the National Health Service stands as a testament to this.

However, there were many forms that a National Health Service could have taken. There must be a question mark over whether the form that it did take was the most radical that it *might* have taken. Perhaps more importantly, was it the most radical that it *could* have taken, given the constraints under which the government was operating?

There is no room here to discuss the lengthy process of negotiation, promises, threats and manoeuvres out of which the NHS was born. It is outlined in *Class Struggle, The State and Medicine*, by V. Navarro. We have touched, in passing, upon Aneurin Bevan's placation of the medical profession in allowing the continuation of private practice within the NHS. This was only one of several compromises. We will return to the question of local control, which was another. David Stark Murray, long-standing president and historian of the Socialist Medical Association, has itemised seven features which were not achieved: no unified service; no occupational health service; no abolition of private practice within the National Health Service; no whole-time salaried service; no decision on the provision of staff committees including every grade of worker; no decision on the composition of hospital management committees; no statement on the need for a district general hospital to serve all sick. Some of these have since been achieved, others we may not now consider desirable.

It was not, however, to be any of these items that was to prove the first and most crucial test of the parliamentary Labour Party's resolve for the new service. Bevan allowed there to be written into the National Health Service a provision for the implementation of charges for services, if a future government was so to require. It is, almost certainly correctly, argued that Bevan himself never intended to make use of this provision. However, when the Labour Party was returned to power on a slim majority after the general election of 1950, it was faced with the familiar prospect of economic crisis; but also with a demand for certain services, spectacles, drugs and dental treatment, which exceeded the levels that had been anticipated five years earlier.

Ideologically, the most important feature of the NHS had been that it was free at the time of use. By imposing prescription charges of up to one shilling (5p), as the Labour government did in 1951, it was undermining this basic socialist tenet. To his credit, Bevan resigned from the Labour government on this issue, as too did Harold Wilson, although as he later declared, for him 'It was a practical problem. Nye saw it more as an issue of principle.'

The Labour government faced a decision all too familiar to Labour governments of the future. How far was it prepared to push ahead with socialist transformation at a time when it was also charged with the management of a capitalist economy? Unfortunately, it fell at the first fence. It got up to stumble on, but fences and politicians have been tumbling ever since.

1951–73: Stagnation   The 1950s were the period when we were told that we had 'never had it so good'. For some of 'us' this was, of course, very true. At a time when industrialists in other countries were embarking upon massive post-war reconstruction programmes, with financiers agreeing to take comparatively low returns on capital while they reinvested to modernise, Britain became the source of easy profits. The biggest single asset-stripping exercise in history was taking place under 14 years of Conservative patronage. Much of the profit was carried abroad, as the emerging and enlargening multinationals used their intricate accounting procedures to shift capital round the globe or, receiving little discouragement, quite openly exported it. Some of the profit stayed at home. A little was used to eliminate the worst of pre-war hardships, but most was used to give the appearance of prosperity. People were urged to consume more and more luxury goods, and British advertising, spurred on by the emerging commercial television, found ingenious ways of conjuring up new 'needs', that people never knew they had. But behind the boom, the economic fabric was crumbling.

That the Conservative Party should benignly supervise this process is understandable. The class interests that it represents were doing very nicely out of it. As soon as one artificial boom was over another could always be found, or so it seemed at the time. The process reached its zenith in the late sixties when a boom was created from, of all things, empty property. That the Labour Party should fail to see what was going on was unforgivable. It deluded itself that old-style, class politics were over. The post-war period was the period of the ascent of social democracy. Latter-day rising stars of the Labour Party, many of whom have subsequently defected to the Social Democratic Party, can with some justification claim that that the forces emerging within the Labour Party now have little in common with the Labour Party of the fifties and sixties that they treated as their own personal possession. It is perhaps understandable that they could then argue that class divisions in British society had ended, equipping themselves with the writings of Anthony Crosland and theses of the 'new managerialism'. It is hardly credible that they could still believe it. The sad but important consequence for the National Health Service was that the 1950s and 1960s were decades in which it was ideologically deserted and allowed to fall back onto its own defences.

Without a Labour Party, nor any other political party of any national significance, prepared to fight for socialism there was nobody to defend the ideal of a national health service. Matters of real ideological importance were argued as purely practical issues, in the manner of Harold Wilson's resignation over the introduction of prescription charges. The argument rarely concerned what was best for the health service, but rather what was best for the economy in which it operated. Harold Wilson's very rapid abandonment of socialism, without a hint of a fight, at the behest of the Bank of England and the International Monetary Fund are stories which have been fully told elsewhere. The National Health Service rapidly became one among many components of an ailing capitalist economy. Bits of it, or the whole if need be, were expendable, if the 'health' of the capitalist economy demanded it.

It was not unexpected that the incoming 1952 Tory government should follow the outgoing Labour government in introducing prescription charges of one shilling (5p) a form and charges for dental treatment. It was able to raise £20 million, reducing the cost of the service and transferring this sum 'elsewhere'. The charges were raised to one shilling (5p) per item at the end of 1956 and two shillings (10p) per item in 1961. To its credit, the incoming Labour government of 1964 abolished the charges, fulfilling a manifesto pledge, but shortly reneged, reintroducing them in 1968. But where then were the Aneurin Bevans, prepared to resign rather than be a party to this important ideological reverse?

Some charges for health care have been, and still are, perhaps more of an issue of ideological significance than practical importance for the National Health Service. The same cannot be said for the state of hospital buildings. We will in the second half of this chapter be implicitly questioning whether it was right for the NHS to be so firmly based upon hospitalised medicine. However, rightly or wrongly, both the Labour and the Conservative plans for the National Health Service included the district general hospital as central. Despite this, only one general hospital was constructed in the first 17 years of the NHS. The 1962 Hospital Building Programme was aimed at putting an end to this. And the next 10 years did see very real increases in spending devoted to hospital building, reaching a peak of £393 million in 1972. But this was very far short of what was needed to stem the decay which had, literally, been rotting away hospital buildings for a long time preceding and including the 15 years of the NHS. David Owen, as Minister of Health, testified to his sense of shock when, after six years as a medical student, he finally arrived at a hospital which had *not* been built in the ninteenth century.

New hospital buildings may not, as we have seen, be all that they could be, but a substantial portion of the health care of the NHS has been provided within hospital buildings which, constructed one hundred or more years ago, have long outlived what could reasonably be considered a serviceable life time. Many were never intended as hospitals in the first place, being converted workhouses, or the like. To keep such structures in workable repair requires constant injections of resources. This has not been forthcoming; the buildings have fallen into disrepair. An investigation by Nick Davidson, in the *Times Health Supplement* of 20 November 1981, reported on the extent to which present-day hospital buildings, including a number which *have* been built recently, are in need of repair. The investigation reported also the extreme unlikelihood of the necessary repairs being performed. It has been the appalling condition of many of the buildings of the National Health Service that has made it so easy for health authorities to effect closures, implementing the programmes of cuts, which formed the next cycle in the spiral of deterioration.

1973–?: The cuts   You could have been excused in the early 1970s for believing that the era of commitment to the National Health Service had finally arrived. The Hospital Building Programme, albeit in a somewhat diluted version from its original 1962 form, was now beginning to produce a number of new district general hospitals. Even a few purpose built health centres, which had been envisaged by socialists as the cornerstone of general practice under the NHS were being opened. Nurses, albeit after campaigns of unprecedented militancy, received a meaningful wage rise for the first time ever. Hospital ancillary workers and medical technicians, also after widespread industrial action, received less in the way of cash but served notice that they were no longer prepared to be the weak and compliant recipients of insultingly low pay. Some of the concessions to the NHS had been wrung out of the incoming 1974 Labour government, mindful no doubt of the reasons for the fall of the previous Tory administration.

The return of the Labour government might have been expected to herald a renaissance for the National Health Service. Incoming Labour governments had previously scrapped health charges and embarked upon programmes of public expenditure. The Labour Party of the mid-1970s was, however, little different from its predecessor Labour Party of the late 1960s. Rather than embark upon a revitalised socialist programme, it merely picked up the reins where the Conservatives had left off.

On reflection, it seems that the historic role of the Heath government of 1970–74 was to lay down the agenda for government in the 1970s, an agenda which was to be followed without significant alteration by Labour governments. The Barber mini-budget of 1973 was the first in a long series of deflationary budgets which, much too late, recognised the appalling condition of the British economy, which had been bled dry. They aimed to revitalise it, at the expense of the public sector and the living conditions of the working class generally. Successive Labour budgets were constructed from the same mould.

The Conservative government created another policy tool, applicable to the National Health Service, which was to be taken up by the incoming Labour government and was to prove an important vehicle by which cuts could be implemented. This was the reorganisation of the administrative machinery of the NHS.

The administration of the National Health Service was sorely in need of overhaul. Prior to 1974, the health service was composed of three seperate arms: the hospital sector, the community services and the general practitioner sevices. The hospital services were administered by a patchy amalgam of regional hospital boards and hospital management committees for non-teaching hospitals and boards of governors for teaching hospitals. Community services were administered directly by the local authorities. And the general practitioner services had a number of executive councils to administer general medical practitioners, dental practitioners, etc. It was all a bit of a mess born out of the many compromises and vested interests that had to be accounted for in the original NHS Act.

The absence of a unified service was the first of the seven features that the Socialist Medical Association had listed as deficiencies in the NHS. It was agreed by all parties that this 'tripartite' structure should be ended. However, what was to replace it should have caused far more discussion and disagreement than it did.

The Conservative Secretary of State for Social Services, Sir Keith Joseph, called in an American based management consultancy firm, the McKinsey Corporation, to advise him on the structure that the service should take. Not surprisingly, their recommendations, which were largely adopted by the Conservatives, were designed to ensure tight, hierarchical managerial control. Patients, as it was later put, were considered to be 'not part of the organisation'. The interest of the patients was to be represented in a toothless watchdog called a community health council. The composition of this was a peculiar patchwork of interests sufficiently chaotically constituted to match its virtual total absence of power. In a number of cases, community health councils have proved to be important focal points for the rallying of public opposition to the cuts, and raising of fundamental questions about the nature of health care delivery. But this has been the product of the individual interests and energies of particular CHC members and the extent of wider mobilisation, rather than a product of their design, which if anything would seem to guarantee their impotence.

To their extreme discredit, the incoming Labour government picked up and introduced the Tory administrative proposals virtually intact. In so doing, they were accepting a fundamental tenet of the McKinsey proposals that matters of health care delivery were non-political issues. The National Health Service was not to be administered in the way that was normally adopted for political policy areas, such as housing or even education, via a local elected structure. It was to be administered in a way that was designed to be 'managerially efficient'. Barbara Castle, the incoming Minister of Health, offered some compromises, increasing the number of local authority members, but argued that it was impossible, so late in the day, to make any fundamental changes. But in adopting the basic proposals the Labour government was contributing to the removal of politics from the decision-making sector of the health services. What they might have done, had they been concerned with creating a socialist health service, we will return to in a later chapter. They succeeded in producing a bureaucratic machine, which was to demonstrate its efficiency, but only in pushing through the programme of cuts that was in the pipeline.

The whole sad story of the recent dismantling of the National Health Service has been well documented elsewhere. A number of individual struggles of resistance have become legendary testimonies to both the resolve of local people and to the resolve of health administrators in pushing through cuts no matter what might stand in their path. The Elizabeth Garrett Anderson Hospital, Hounslow Hospital, Bethnal Green Hospital and others have focused public attention on the local impact of central government policy. Patients have been seen being bundled unwillingly into cars and ambulances, wards have been seen to be vandalised by the departing administration to avoid their occupation and operation under the control of members of the workforce and the local community. These have been the dramatic closures. But for every case that has met this sort of resistance there have been dozens that have quietly gone down. After maybe a token gesture of protest—the community health council invoking its statutory power of delay, the workers negotiating an improvement in their own job prospects or redundancy terms— large numbers of NHS facilities have succumbed to the inevitable. This is not just the inevitable outcome of government policy of the last 10 years, over which the programme has been implemented, but of government policy of the last 35 years, over which important components of the service have been so underfinanced as to leave many of the facilities in such a state of physical disrepair that it is very hard for anyone to mount a rational argument for their preservation.

An exception to this rule is the Thornbury Children's Annexe in Sheffield. A report on health services in Sheffield wrote of it:

> This is the largest medical unit in the city and contains most of the Children's Hospital's medical beds. Its closure would seriously prevent the Children's Hospital from providing a comprehensive service. It is a specialist centre for the care of children with spina bifida and hydrocephalus, and it contains the isolation

unit. This is important because it means that children in the hospital who develop an infectious disease do not have to be moved to a different hospital with new medical and nursing staff, and dislocation of their treatment. Its facilities are unique in Sheffield and invaluable, especially in working out treatment schedules for diabetic children.

There are no horror stories of cockroaches in the kitchens, flaking paint in the operating theatres, porters staggering up stairs with patients because the lifts are always out of order. Everyone speaks of the excellent standards of care and the 'ideal' location for children. Despite this, Thornbury is closing. Thornbury is closing because of a programme of 'rationalisation' of paediatric services in Sheffield. Paediatric medical beds are over-provided, despite waiting lists for paediatric surgery. The Thornbury Annexe is a 'luxury'. Its superb, but somewhat remote, location makes it comparatively expensive to run.

Initially, plans to close the Thornbury Annexe met strong resistance. Important and influential medical staff opposed the closure. They have since been offered more prestigious facilities elsewhere. Full time nursing staff, who also fought the closure, have been offered alternative jobs and replaced by staff on short-term contracts. After twice successfully fighting off plans for closure, the 'Save Thornbury Campaign' has, faced with a third plan, been drained of energy and some of the key groups essential in its former resistance. Only a few local trades unionists and the Sheffield District Trades Council offered any fight at the last stand. Thornbury Children's Annexe is now doomed to close.

The story of Thornbury Annexe is only exceptional in respect of its state of good repair. In other respects it is illustrative. It illustrates the waste of valuable facilities and the lengths to which administrators are being driven as they are forced by central government to take apart the services under their control. Why is it going on?

The simple answer is that it is going on because we are shackled to an economic system which has long outrun its efficiency. Governments at the helm have attempted to pump money into the private industrial sector in the vain hope that they can recreate profitability to get us out of the mess that too much industrial profitability got us into. We are now picking up the tab for the milking of profits in the 1950s and 1960s. The NHS like other parts of the public sector is being expected to foot the bill.

At the same time as being starved of resources the National Health

Service is expected to do more, as the ailing economy produces an additional load of social casualties and as an ageing population increases the numbers of elderly people. We will be considering in the next chapter how the service might be expanded to meet people's real needs. Financial starvation is one force keeping the service firmly on its current path. There are, however, other forces, inside the health service, which militate against any radical reorientation.

The National Health Service as a repair service for capitalism

The National Health Service has been overwhelmed by the capitalist economic system in ways other than the manner and the extent to which it is funded. To argue that the NHS has been systematically underfinanced is not simply to argue for additional money to be spent on more of the same. One of the most beneficial outcomes of a number of the struggles that have arisen around the closure of existing NHS facilities, in particular the fight against the closure of the Elizabeth Garrett Anderson Hospital in London, is that in the course of those struggles attention has turned towards the *nature* of health care delivery and questions have been asked about why the health service has come to take the form that it has.

A characterisation of the National Health Service Cecil Foggitt, when I spoke to him before starting to write this book, told me that he had only gone into a general practice in Attercliffe as a temporary measure. As a socialist medic he was anticipating the transformation of health care that the new National Health Service would bring. He expected very quickly to see the end of doctor-orientated practice and the creation of teams of practitioners operating from new health centres. One reason that these centres were never built is the story of under-financing that we have been telling. Another is the resistance of general practitioners, who clung to their ideological attachment to independence. It is also the story of how patterns of health care go deeper into the nature of the economic and social system. The health care we get, and the way that we get it, reflect this system.

Our system of health care delivery is hierarchical; it is sexist; it is racist. These are strong accusations. I will justify them in reverse order.

We have briefly considered how the NHS fails to respond to the needs of ethnic minorities. It is, on the other hand, extremely reliant upon, and exploits, their labour. A trip round virtually any hospital in a major metropoitan area will reveal a marked overrepresentation of ethnic minority members among the cleaning staff and doing the preparatory work in the kitchens. It takes a whole army of ancillary and domestic staff to run a large institution like a hospital. These badly paid, unglamorous and often hazardous jobs would go unfilled were it not for the presence of ethnic minority labour—even in the current economic recession.

But aren't black workers also present further up the health service's hierarchy, among the nurses and medical staff? There is a fair representation of ethnic minorities among nurses and doctors, but here also they occupy the lower status, lower pay jobs. Recent changes in nursing have produced a more professional structure. Very few black nurses occupy the senior managerial positions. Black doctors, likewise, are overrepresented in junior medical positions. As you move up through the very distinct hierarchy of the medical profession from senior house officer to consultant, the percentage of overseas-born doctors drops from over 50 per cent to less than 16 per cent. And as you scan the medical specialties, from the less glamorous geriatric and psychiatric medicine to the more glamorous general medicine and surgery, an equivalent drop-off is found. Black doctors rarely occupy positions which qualify for the highly lucrative distinction awards made by the DHSS which can, at the top end, bring supplementary payments of about £15,000 a year.

A similar picture can be painted with respect to women employees in the NHS. An unfortunate result of the introduction of a better career structure for the nursing profession is an increased likelihood of the minority of male nurses occupying the top nursing posts. It is ironic to note that the trade union to which most unionised nurses belong, the Confederation of Health Service Employees, has an all-male national executive. The general secretary, Albert Spanswick, is himself a former male nurse. The Royal Commission on the National Health Service, which reported in 1979, did not tabulate the occupational position of women doctors, as it did doctors born overseas, although it did offer the following comment:

> In the circumstances, it is not surprising that in England in 1978 only about 10 per cent of consultants were women, against 16 per cent of GPs and 54 per cent of doctors working in the community health service. Over 40 per cent of medical assistants in hospitals are women, in a grade for which a fellowship or equivalent is not normally required, and which contains many doctors specialising in paediatrics, obstetrics and gynaecology.

The absence of adequate representation of blacks and women at

the top end of the professional structures within the NHS is important, not only because there is an unfair distribution of pay and career
prospects, but also because there is an unfair distribution of power.
Unlike almost any other professional hierarchy, to occupy a senior
medical position within the health services confers a large measure of
control over the direction of those services.

The dominance of the medical profession   Medics defend their
control over the health services jealously. The arguable claim that
doctors must be guaranteed clinical autonomy, the power to control
the treatment of an individual patient in the way that they at the time
judge best, is translated, by sleight of hand, into a totally unjustifiable
claim for complete professional autonomy, the power to control all
aspects of the management and direction of everything remotely
associated with the patient. In effect that means control over the
whole of the National Health Service. The district management
team, functionally the most important unit within the health service,
is comprised of three doctors, two administrators and a nurse—see
diagram 3. For non-medics to challenge the proposal of a doctor,
they must be prepared to counter the combined weight of the medical
personnel who are quick to form alliances against 'outside' interfer-
ence. Despite successive government commitments, both Labour
and Tory, to the expansion of community care, the proportion of
NHS finances directed into acute medical services has increased
continually throughout the life of the NHS. When it comes to taking
decisions about how the money is actually going to be spent, doctors,
and particularly those from the more prestigious sections, control the
positions that matter.

The top male consultant is a self-perpetuating breed. The educational ladder that leads to entry into the medical profession is a prime
example of how the class that dominates can reproduce its domination in the next generation. How many parents of working class girls
in their early teens consider channelling them down the highly restric-
tive educational path which might, if they successfully clear all the
hurdles, lead them to become a consultant in open heart surgery? To
enter a medical school you must have the right A-levels, normally at
very high grades. To study for those A-levels requires that you have
already successfully completed the appropriate O-levels. It all starts
at a very early age. Not only is the bias against starting on the route
very marked; there are also different opportunities of successfully
jumping all the hurdles. Even with the right A-levels, which are
obtained more easily with a supportive home environment, entry into

Diagram 3. The services under the control of the district management team.

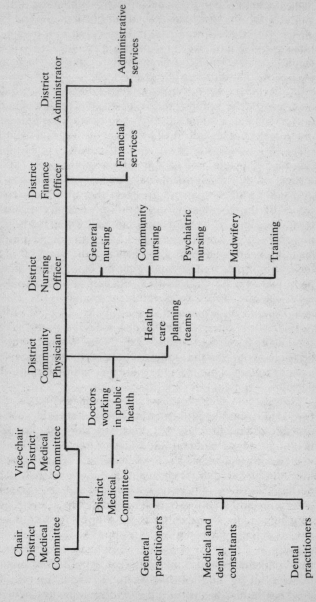

District Management Team

medical school is by no means automatic. If your father (or rarely, your mother) attended a particular medical school your chances of entry are greatly improved. Even better still if you play rugby!

The restricted educational path is not only selective in determining who will successfully pass along it; it is selective in terms of the material that is taught—the system of ideas and the view of the world that is passed down from one generation of doctors to the next. The medical view of the patient is very slanted. It is the unavoidable outcome of an education which has taught the practitioner to reduce all aspects of the world to conventional scientific analysis.

The medical view of the patient treats him or her as an isolated individual, separable into a kit of parts, which can then be individually treated in abstraction from the person as a whole. This view is crystallised in the detailed medical specialties that exist. The 'case' in bed 1 is a ruptured ulcer; the 'case' in bed 2 a defective kidney. Medical training specifically inhibits doctors from adopting a view of ill-health as socially created (some aspects of which were outlined in chapter two). Doctors see their own role as being to treat the symptoms; rarely will they be concerned with causes. The more dramatic the symptoms are, the more will be the kudos, and the financial incentives associated with the cure. Within the medical profession acclamation is for those who accomplish the technically excellent, not for those who can tackle the commonplace, although the latter may be responsible for alleviating far greater suffering.

The medical profession controls the funding of medical research. It is powerful in determining the size of the cake and its distribution. It will be directed towards those areas that doctors collectively deem to be important.

The consequences of medical domination   Before going further, let me set one possible misconception straight. I am not opposed to medical practice which is technically excellent. I sincerely hope that if I am ever in need of acute medical attention I shall be able to get the best that the National Health Service is able to provide. In fact I should like to see good medical attention made more available and more equitably distributed. I should like to see a steelworker in Sheffield able to obtain, under the NHS, the best that is available to the city gent that lives in close proximity to London's several teaching hospitals.

My concern is with the implication of medical dominance for decision-making, and with the implication of its partial view of illness, health and health care for priorities and policies within the

NHS. The women's movement has drawn attention to the current orientation of the health services. It has been the experience of women that the dominant medical view of the patient has failed to acknowledge what have been women's major problems. Indeed, the way that medical care has usually been delivered, by authoritarian, dogmatic, patronising, remote male doctors, and the low priority given to the caring services have in many respects intensified these problems. 'Our bodies, ourselves' is not just a slogan expressing the fact that in many cases women have developed collective knowledge which is far better at tackling the problems they experience than conventional medical wisdom; it is a reclamation of the whole person from a medical system which has broken it up into parts and treated each one in dehumanised isolation from the rest.

The women's movement has identified two things, in particular, about the western technologically-orientated medical view. It adopts a view of the body as a machine and it decries the importance of collective experience and collective action. We have dwelt on the former in considering the nature of medical education. But there is one important consequence that we have not yet considered. This is the implication for alternative modes of treatment. These have been outlawed. Holistic therapies, homeopathy, acupuncture—therapies which involve looking at the whole person and his or her environment—these have been virtually excluded from the National Health Service. 'Fringe' medicine *is* an area where charlatans have been able to exploit people, callously offering unsubstantiatable claims for their therapy programmes. But does this distinguish it quite so markedly from mainstream medicine? It has been its privileged position, rather than any partiular claim to healing ability, that has enabled mainstream, hospital-centred, medicine to resist the encroachment of anything that threatened its position of control. This is unfortunate; the alternative approach is something from which the health service may have much to gain.

The women's movement has shown also the need for a collective social approach to problems of ill-health. Conventional medicine teaches us to think of our health problems as our own individual problems. We are often blamed, implicitly or explicitly, for ill-health which has its origin in the social roles that we fill, or·in our personal rejection of these roles. Women, in particular, have suffered from this. We have discussed in an earlier chapter the social roots of much of the illness that we experience. Individualised medicine makes no systematic attempt to treat, or even expose, these roots. The individual is treated when attention ought to be directed towards the individual's social experience. The awareness that the social experience is producing ill-health will normally indicate that the correct remedial action is social action.

The oft-cited analogy of a national repair service is a good one. The casualties of the hazardous social system are wheeled in to the health services to have their faulty parts patched up, only to be returned to their slot in the same system which continues unchanged. The hospital is the automobile repair centre located alongside a frantic motorway. Where the analogy falls down is that we normally demand more control over our car mechanics than over our doctors. From the perspective of the medical profession the situation is analogised in the story of the physician on the river bank, described by J. B. McKinlay in 'A case for refocusing upstream':

'You know', he said, 'sometimes it feels like this. There I am standing by the shore of a swiftly flowing river and I hear the cry of a drowning man. So I jump into the river, put my arms around him, pull him to the shore and apply artificial respiration. Just when he begins to breathe, there is another cry for help. So I jump into the river, reach him, pull him to shore, apply artificial respiration, and then just as he begins to breathe, another cry for help. So back in the river again, reaching, pulling, applying, and then another yell. Again and again, without end, goes the sequence. You know, I am so busy jumping in, pulling them to shore, applying artificial respiration that I have no time to see who the hell is upstream pushing them all in.'

The social background of the majority of medical practitioners leaves them oblivious to the upstream social existence of their patients. For the few that are drawn from the same social background as their working class patients years of isolating medical training will have thrown it well to the backs of their minds. It is not surprising if they themselves recreate the next generation of medical practitioners in the same style.

Dominance of the medical view of ill-health affects not only the way that medical practitioners view their own role, nor only the way that the public views their role. It also conditions the way that other health workers view themselves and are viewed by society. The caring function is relegated as the curing function is promoted. In reality, the real successes have been in the former area, although the accolades have been directed towards the latter.

The role of medicine   The defence that most medical practitioners offer for the rejection of alternative modes of treatment is that they are unproven. The medical profession though is more than a little reluctant to hold its own practices up for historical scrutiny. They are right to be nervous. Many accepted medical procedures would fail to stand close inspection.

Thomas McKeown, formerly professor of social medicine at the University of Birmingham, has examined the substance behind some of the claims which have been made on behalf of medical interventions. The near eradication of respiratory tuberculosis has, for example, often been attributed to treatment by drugs (chemotherapy) and the introduction of BCG vaccination. Inspection of the record of the annual death-rate from respiratory tuberculosis—see diagram 4—tells a different story. These two medical interventions were only, in reality, responsible for clearing up the tail end of a disease which was already dramatically on the decline. This decline was the product of improvements in social conditions: the quality of the water supply, the disposal of waste and sewerage, and general conditions of living. McKeown examined a number of diseases in his book *The Role of Medicine* and considered for each the contribution of medical interventions. It was generally less than medical mythology would hold.

It follows, that if medical procedures in the past haven't had all the effects that have been attributed to them, we might also do well to scrutinise medical procedures currently in use. Professor Archie Cochrane, in a famous Rock Carling lecture given in 1971, subsequently published as *Effectiveness and Efficiency in the Health Services*, advocated that this should be done by fuller use of the evaluative randomised control trial technique. The randomised control trial is a mechanism by which a group of patients suffering from a particular disease is randomly divided into two sub-groups. One sub-group is administered the treatment under study. The other is administered no treatment or a placebo treatment, one which is known to have no positive or negative effect. Sometimes the new treatment will be tested against a treatment which is already in use. The progress of the two sub-groups is monitored and compared.

Systematic analysis of the value of a number of surgical procedures currently routinely employed suggests that they are often carried out more from custom or fashion, than because of their proven therapeutic value. One such procedure is tonsillectomy, the removal of (normally) a child's tonsils. In some areas, this operation is carried out virtually as a matter of course on healthy children; in other areas, its

Diagram 4
Respiratory tuberculosis: mean annual death-rates (standardised to 1901 population) for England and Wales

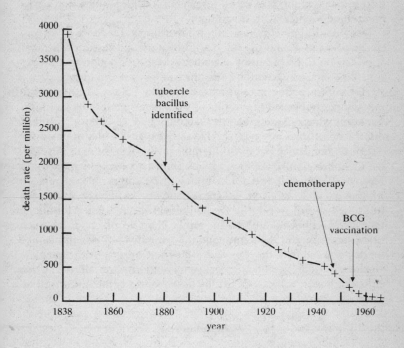

Source: T. McKeown, *The Role of Medicine*, Oxford: Basil Blackwell 1979, p. 92.

use is reserved for situations where it is demanded only by the doctor's interpretation of a patient's clinical condition. A study conducted in Vermont, USA, in 1973, revealed that the probability of having a tonsillectomy before one's twenty-first birthday was 66 per cent in one area and between 16 per cent and 22 per cent in all the surrounding areas. Tonsillectomy is a minor operation, but not pleasant and occasionally hazardous. The Radical Statistics Health Group estimated that possibly as many as eight children a year die as a result of it in the United Kingdom.

A similar question mark hangs over the use of surgery for a hernia. The Radical Statistics Health Group in its pamphlet *In Defence of the NHS* reports that 'it seems that an average 65-year-old man with a hernia runs four times the risk of dying if he opts for surgery, rather than wearing a truss and running the risk of strangulation'. The Group lists a number of other surgical procedures which can hardly be justified when held up to scrutiny.

Most medical practitioners are not charlatans. Evidence of corrupt practice usually brings the full disapproval of a profession which has good reason to be proud of its name. It is the exception that proves the rule—such an exception being the case of the intra uterine device (IUD) contraceptive known as the Dalkon Shield. An American practitioner published the results of what he claimed to be an objective study which showed that the Dalkon Shield was 'better' in almost every respect than other IUDs. He did not declare that he held the patent on the device nor a considerable financial stake in its development. Subsequently the device was shown to make a number of women sterile; and was often found to be impossible to remove without complicated and dangerous surgery. Although withdrawn from the western world, the Dalkon Shield was marketed for a long time after its effects were known, within Third World countries. Such stories are rare, but their consequences for individual patients can be so devastating that they must be guarded against with complete vigilance. Medical and surgical interventions are all too often embarked upon without their full consequences being known, particularly to the patient.

Summary

We looked, historically, in the first half of this chapter at how the National Health Service has been consistently under-financed, with successive Labour and Conservative governments using the NHS as one of the components of public spending which were to be turned off and on to suit the regulation of the British capitalist economy. As Labour governments in particular have found, the ship of the economy has a momentum of its own which normally leads *it* to control the helm. Without a serious challenge to the capitalist superstructure this situation must remain unchanged.

Underfinancing has been a cause of deterioration in the NHS, which, as we have seen in the previous chapter has been all too readily exploited by a private sector hovering like birds of carrion on the perimeter. One reason why it has often been difficult to launch a defence of the National Health Service has been because of the limited nature of the health care available within it. This we have examined in the second half of this chapter. Domination of health care by the medical profession and the medical view of health and ill-health has provided neither the opportunity nor the resources for a serious 'refocusing upstream', which would allow more adequate recognition of the caring role of the health service, and that the root of much ill-health lies in the capitalist nature of British society.

5.

Broadening the Scope of the National Health Service

The services provided under the National Health Service owe more to historical accident than to purposeful design. The National Health Service Act, under which it was created, brought together existing health services. Subsequent revisions to the NHS have, to all intents and purposes, been merely internal restructurings. They may have given greater prominence to one area; attempted to direct finances towards another; but at no time has there been a fundamental reappraisal of the range and balance of services provided.

The move towards a socialist health service, a service which is an integral part of a socialist society, or, in the first instance, the movement to create such a society, must start from such a fundamental reappraisal. We have argued that the health services currently provided are the product of a socialist potential systematically distorted by the dynamics of the capitalist social and economic system. A health service that formed part of the movement to transform this system could not be content with simply 'mopping up' after it. It would seek to deliver health services in a way that would both prefigure the society in the making—that is, incorporate as much future socialist health care as possible—and actively combat the society on the decline.

An occupational health service

For socialists, the arena which has longest been perceived as the most blatant reflection of the uncaring and exploitative nature of the capitalist system has been the point of production—the workplace. Over recent years, the struggle against capitalism has broadened into other areas, such as housing, the environment, sex roles, and race. The prime characteristic of a capitalist economy is the relationship between the people that produce the wealth of that economy and the people who control, manage and profit from that production. This is not in any sense to relegate other struggles to secondary importance, but to recognise where, historically, the principal confrontation against capitalism has arisen. The longest standing item on the socialist 'shopping list' for services for health has been an occupational health service.

Support for such a service has been widespread over the last 35 years. The Socialist Medical Association was calling for a comprehensive occupational health service long before, and at the time that, the National Health Service was created. It was second on the list of items the SMA regretted had not been achieved by the original National Health Service Act. Such a service was recommended by the Dale Commission, which reported in 1951. In 1958 the Labour Party promised legislation if it came to power. Subsequently, TUC and Labour Party conference resolutions have called for 'a comprehensive occupational health service as part of the National Health Service'.

Despite all this recognition of the need for a proper health service centred on the place of work, current provision is patchy in the extreme. Existing legislative demands on industry are minimal: all companies employing more than 11 workers should provide first aid boxes and have available some member of the workforce with first aid training, and a limited number of regulations which specify regular medical checkups for employees engaged in certain hazardous occupations, e.g. lead smelting. Beyond this, what is provided by a company is optional. In 1976 the Employment Medical Advisory Service conducted a survey of industry 'to provide a general view of the current situation regarding the provision of occupational health services in Great Britain as a whole'. Some of the findings of this survey were summarised by the Trade Union Research Unit in its report *The Need for an Occupational Health Service*, in the following terms:

* that 85 per cent of the firms in the sample employing some 34 per cent of the workforce provided no occupational health service other than workers with responsibility for first aid, but employed for less than 10 hours a week in that capacity;
* that only 0.5 per cent of the firms employing 16.5 per cent of the workforce in the sample provided full time medical and nursing staff;
* that the remaining 49 per cent of the workforce in the sample

were covered by various combinations of part time medical and
nursing staff.

Current provision is clearly inadequate, both in terms of the numbers
of workers for whom services are provided and the level of the
services themselves. The situation will remain largely unchanged, or
actually worsen in the current economic climate, as long as provision
is a voluntary duty upon employers. What *would* be provided if the
plans of organisations such as the Socialist Medical Association (now
the Socialist Health Association) were implemented?

Against the background of major and minor accidents that was
noted when considering the relationship of employment to health in
chapter two, it is unavoidable that a prime function of an occupational health service will be the provision of first aid. The need for this
has intensified over recent years. A major 'casualty' of the cuts in the
National Health Service has been the provision of accident and
emergency services; and a major response to the recession in industry
has been the lowering of safety standards. A proper workplace
accident service would not only concern itself with the treatment of
those accidents that do not require immediate hospital attention but
would also provide full monitoring of the occurrence of accidents to
highlight the presence of dangerous machinery and industrial processes.

Monitoring is equally important with respect to the second function of a comprehensive occupational health service—the medical
surveillance of the workforce. We also noted the technical difficulties
of identifying a number of the most frequently recurring occupational
diseases, when we looked at the relationship between employment
and health. These difficulties can only be overcome by fuller monitoring. Individual general practices still record the occupation of patients only in the minority of cases. Their separate unlinked record
systems mean that, even where occupations are recorded, it is impossible to build up a health picture of the whole of a particular
workforce. Such a picture could be constructed if workers' health
records were also kept at the workplace and, of course, systematically analysed. Were proper individual monitoring conducted, it would
allow the earliest treatment of numerous conditions which are comparatively minor if treated quickly, but serious if allowed to degener-
ate; it would allow the identification of workers at special risk because of their work situation; and it would allow attention to be
drawn towards hazardous processes *before* their toll reached
epidemic proportions. Such monitoring should not be restricted to

purely clinical information, that is physiological and biological measures. The importance of the workers' subjective evaluation has been stressed by a group of Italian health workers:

First, the workers possess first-hand knowledge of the working environment derived from direct experience. Second, exposure, prior to causing harm (latency) causes discomfort: irritative complaints, psychosomatic reactions, psychological changes such as sense of danger, insecurity, etc. The only reliable measure of these conditions, which gives an early indication of the presence of risk, is the person who experiences them, particularly when, as in the case of working environments, s/he is one of a group.

They have advocated the adoption of a 'homogenous worker group register' which would include as an important component individual workers' own feelings about their working environment and their own perception of their health. Such perceptions are the major basis upon which it is possible to monitor the stress induced by patterns and types of work.

In order that the monitoring of individual workers can also be used to identify particularly hazardous working conditions, the occupational health service should maintain full records of those conditions under which they work. Such environmental monitoring of the workplace should be conducted by properly trained industrial hygienists who can relate their findings back to the health experiences of the workers.

The question of who should control the occupational health service is the vital one. Employers have shown an interest in workforce monitoring where this can be used to exclude sections of the workforce who may be identifiably at risk, such as pregnant women, rather than removing the hazards. Where occupational health services do currently exist, pre-employment testing is one of their major functions. As well as being used to exclude women from some jobs, they have also recently found that black workers have a lower average number of white blood cells, possibly making them more vulnerable to chemical pollutants. The racist and sexist implications are clear. (They're also 'in their own best interest, you must understand!'). If a particular process is especially hazardous to any section of the workforce it must be potentially hazardous to all sections of the workforce. Proper environmental and personal monitoring, under the control of the workforce, would focus attention on the process of work, where that attention rightly belongs, rather than on sections of the workforce.

Related to this, of course, is the question of who should pay for the occupational health service. Failure to resolve this may have been the major reason for the absence of an occupational health service in the original plan for the NHS. If the state, via the NHS, pays for the service, doesn't this allow the employers to shift some of their costs onto the state and shrug off responsibility for the health of the workforce? This formed the substance of the argument between Ernest Bevin, Labour government Minister of Labour, and the TUC General Council as far back as 1945. This is partly a problem of financing, which doesn't raise any more difficulty than, say, state-run employment training schemes; partly a problem of adequate supportive legislation; but most importantly a problem of control—control over the occupational health service and its power to turn findings into control over the workplace.

The current system is haphazard, inadequate where it is provided, and works to the very real disadvantage of the workers. The demand for a proper occupational health service must remain high on the list of reforms necessary to redirect the NHS back to the interests of working people.

Towards a community focus

Concrete proposals have been formulated for an occupational health service because of the long-standing recognition of the relationship between employment and health. A not unnatural question to ask is what would be the consequence of applying the sort of approach embodied in an occupational health service to the other areas of the capitalist social and economic system that impinge directly on people's health. Do we also need a housing health service, a nutritional health service? The answer is yes, and no.

We do need an approach to the delivery of health care that recognises the social dimensions in the chain of events that lead to ill-health. It would be wrong to specifically select housing, diet, or any other particular aspect for separate study. It could be argued that even singling out occupation will fail to draw attention to the interaction of employment with those other aspects of capitalism that produce ill-health. However, patterns of employment do produce a number of highly specific hazards associated with particular substances or processes. The situation is less clear, as we have earlier argued, regarding housing, for example.

Tom Heller, in *Restructuring the Health Service*, has explored 'the possibilities for a re-orientation of the National Health Service towards a "whole community" approach'. In particular, he has argued for a *community diagnosis* which might involve the following components:

(1) Who is ill, and with what disease in the community?
(2) What might be causing this illness?
(3) What do people do when they are ill?
(4) What facilities and organisations are currently provided for preventing and coping with illness?

These ideas are important and potentially very powerful. They are important because the recognition of community ill-health, informed by the perspective that we have outlined earlier, specifically starts from a very different conception of illness than the individualistic approach we have criticised as being characteristic of the modern western medical view. They could be powerful, because if we recognise the existence of community ill-health, we can also consider the provision of community services or, better still, embark upon programmes of community prevention.

Such ideas are not of course totally new. It was the recognition of the community dimension to illness that led in the last century to the improvement in water supplies, sanitation and disposal of sewerage and in this century to the Clean Air Acts. But these were specific responses to specific events: the discovery, via the cholera epidemics of 1831, 1848–49 and 1854, of the water-borne nature of some diseases; the recognition, following the smogs of 1952, 1959 and 1962, of the unhealthy effects of air pollution. The establishment of a community approach to ill-health would incorporate in a systematic way some of the ideas in these 'one-off' discoveries. In the same way that an occupational health service would exist to deliver immediate first aid, monitor individual health and ill-health experiences, and monitor the working environment in the occupational setting, a community health service would carry out similar functions in the non-occupational setting.

The report of the Black Working Party (which was discussed in chapter two) offered some very useful pointers in this direction. Among their specific recommendations were the need to extend nutritional surveillance in relation to health. One would like to add the surveillance of pollution levels, which is currently conducted on a very piecemeal amateurish basis, and the surveillance of housing conditions, which is conducted from time to time but the results of which are normally kept confidential to local authority housing departments and never related to patterns of ill-health. Environmental health departments, under whose auspices such monitoring now falls, are themselves extremely underfinanced, operating with out-dated equipment which makes CT scanners and fibre optics look like something out of Dr Who. Their monitoring lacks teeth, because they are powerless to intervene in the other policy areas that they are monitoring.

As with occupational health services, there is, in relation to community health, a crying need for fuller information. Tom Heller has made the point that 'the information and analysis that is available to [community physicians] . . . primarily concerns the management of the service rather than the health of the community'. This has been illustrated more generally by the Radical Statistics Health Group in its pamphlet *The Unofficial Guide to Official Health Statistics* which comprehensively reviewed official data sources for the National Health Service and found very little that could help you effectively monitor the health of any section of the population.

This deficiency and also, perhaps, the much more serious deficiency in academic research in this area was recognised in the report of a working party which was convened under the auspices of the Unit for the Study of Health Policy, called *Rethinking Community Medicine*. This working party exhorted the re-formation of a 'public health movement', copying the movement which existed in the middle of the last century and out of which grew the Public Health Acts of 1848 and 1875, the first of which established the post of medical officer of health who

> had to be a legally-qualified medical practitioner whose duties included conducting house-to-house searches for infectious disease; removing the sick from overcrowded housing; vaccinating smallpox contacts; inquiring into school and factory conditions; inspecting sanitary improvements schemes; ascertaining the causes of unexpected death and attending meetings of the local Board of Health.

The medical officer of health has been subsequently replaced by the community physician. This was, potentially, the most progressive product of the 1974 reorganisation of the National Health Service. The community physician should have been responsible for conducting what might be called a 'socio-medical audit'—just the sort of monitoring of community needs and local provision of services that could help to push the services in the direction we are advocating. Unfortunately, community physicians have never been given adequate finances, freedom from administrative duties, or adequately trained support staff, nor have they received the support of the other medical disciplines, who are hostile to the community view of ill-health. Under the 1982 mini-reorganisation of the NHS, the number of community physicians is reduced from about 500 to about 400.

It is also doubtful whether the majority of the incumbents of community physician posts have ever seriously wanted to fulfill a proper community monitoring role; and, even more, whether they would have been prepared to involve themselves in the community struggles that a community diagnosis would demand. The discipline of community medicine is, after all, a medical specialty with all the tendency to view 'community problems' as medical problems and the approach to treatment that that implies.

In contrast to the remote stance adopted by the discipline of community medicine, there have been established recently a number of neighbourhood or community health projects. Reviewing the work of a number of these in *Radical Community Medicine* in 1980/1, Helen Rosenthal judged that their 'viability . . . seems to depend on the degree to which the project is rooted in the community'.

The work of each project has varied, depending on the needs of the community in which it is located. The work of the Waterloo health project, which is described by Helen Rosenthal in some detail, included work with the elderly, work with women, advice and information work and an inquiry into a proposed development project. This variety demonstrates the error of trying to impose a view of community health from outside that community. Such community based projects can be of immense value for the information that they provide to others as well as for the immediate benefit to the communities in which they are located.

Community care—in sickness and in health

Community diagnosis, premised by better community surveillance, should promote an extension of health care *in* the community. Community care should not just be available for those who are sick or who are immediately reliant upon the services of others—the elderly, people with mental and physical handicaps. It should be available to those who are well.

The National Health Service currently provides a range of monitoring and developmental services for mothers and children—in the

form of ante-natal, post-natal and child health clinics. The Black
Report has called for an extension of these. It seeks the provision of
free milk, school meals as a right and the abolition of child poverty.
These are important and necessary measures for the health of our
children and our adults of the future. But we should also be trying to
do something for our present generation of adults. We could do well
by starting with the provision of adequate financing to allow the
extension of primary care to the healthy as well as to the ill. And we
should be seeking to bring these services under close community
control, a point we will return to in the next chapter.

We should also consider the provision of adequate financing for
the removal from hospitals and other long-stay institutions of the
many thousands of people who would enjoy a more fulfilling life in
the community. Large numbers of aged people and those with mental
and physical disabilities are living out their lives in cramped and
understaffed NHS institutions merely because of the inadequacy of
resources for their care in the community. Both Conservative and
Labour governments have, in the past, had paper commitments to
the extension of community care. But this has been more as part of a
callous cost-cutting exercise than as a commitment to the well-being
of the particular patients. It *is* possible merely to turn long-stay
patients out into the community, throwing them onto the support of
families and friends, many of whom are themselves in no position to
provide it. Without adequate support services, provision of meals,
home helps, etc. 'community care' is a cynical disguise for penny-
pinching the NHS at the expense of relatives and friends, particularly
women, who take on an extra burden and are forced to give up jobs,
leisure time activities, and live under greater stress. Properly
financed, community care could allow people from institutions to
reclaim meaningful lives of their own in communities to which they
can contribute valuably, rather than being thrust upon them as a
burden to be disposed of in the easiest and cheapest way.

Such recommendations were again contained within the Black
Report. They formed part of the report's district action programmes.
These and other suggestions of the working party were aimed at
amending the fragmentation of policy-making that we have criticised.
Their approach clearly linked health problems, and inequalities in
health, to nutrition, housing and poverty. It can be argued that they
didn't go far enough. But as far as the Conservative government was
concerned they obviously went too far. Perhaps the government was
recognising what has formed the major argument of this book, that

such improvements and innovations are only possible as part of the general move to replace capitalism by a more compassionate society.

The women's health movement

It would be wrong not to acknowledge how much has been learnt about the ways in which health services *might* be organised, as well as the consequences of how they already are, from the practical experiences of the women's health movement.

Historically, women have felt the inadequacy of existing health care because of the special problems that have arisen from their reproductive role. These problems have been largely neglected by the health services. The letters contained in *Maternity: Letters from Working Women*, edited by Margaret Llewelyn Davies, are vivid testimony to the experiences of pregnancy, childbirth and motherhood that filled the adulthood of Victorian and Edwardian working women. The letters in *Maternity* were sent in 1914

> in response to an appeal from Miss Davies for direct experiences . . . in the [Women's Co-operative] Guild's sustained campaign against the Liberal government and local authorities, to improve the virtually non-existent maternal and infant care then available to the poorer woman. (from the introduction by Gloden Dallas).

The use of abortion as a means of birth control, multiple pregnancies leading to a low proportion of live births, high infant sickness and mortality, were the picture of family life around and within which working women were forced to fit paid employment.

The Women's Co-operative Guild campaigned hard for the provision of proper birth control facilities. It must be said however, that their successes probably owed more to concern for the health of the race, via the next generation of children, than for the women themselves. It has been argued that the improvements in childbirth and childcare facilities that were taking place between the first and second world wars stemmed directly from concern about the very poor 'quality' of the recruits that were drafted into the army during the first world war. As the second world war approached, against an ideological background which reached its crudest in Nazi Germany, birth control gave way to family planning, and eugenics, the study of the development of the human race, came to the fore.

Despite this, the second world war promised to be something of a watershed for the position of women in Britain. As women were drafted into the production process, questions of childbirth and child-care took on a new priority. As Jessie Vaughan and Kay Habershaw recalled, 'there were some beautiful babies born during the war'.

After the war women were put firmly back into their place—into the home—halting the advance that was taking place and which might have been expected to accelerate under the National Health Service. It would be wrong to suggest that childbirth and childcare have not improved quite considerably under the NHS. But it would be equally wrong not to appreciate there are some real, and avoidable, inadequacies; particularly in the way the service views the role and position of women.

The National Health Service has failed to meet women's needs in relation to contraception, abortion, pregnancy and childbirth. Lesley Doyal, in *The Political Economy of Health*, has discussed at length the NHS's 'ambivalent attitude towards the provision of contraceptive advice'. Doctors, who are being increasingly called upon to provide contraceptive advice and methods, receive inadequate or non-existent training. Abortion is more freely available than it was, but the 1967 Abortion Act left far too much power in the hands of individual consultants. Consequently, the availability of abortion under the NHS varies wildly from area to area through the country. The actual process of birth, too, 'has been characterised by a struggle between the male-dominated medical profession and female mid-wives for the control of care during pregnancy and childbirth. The battle was, of course, won by the doctors.' Childbirth has become a highly 'medical' affair. It now takes place almost exclusively in hospitals with an unnecessary degree of intervention—births are often induced on Thursdays or Fridays to avoid the inconvenience of a weekend birth. For women, drugged and strapped into position, birth is a process which is done *to* them and of which they feel little part. The medical view of illness has become part of the process of quite healthy birth. A birth is seen as a symptom which must be treated.

Treatment of the individual in isolation from his or her environment, which literally starts at birth, characterises the medical view of the mental health of women—another area of NHS failing. The rise in the dispensing of tranquillisers has been alarming. Women who are unable to cope with the double burden of domestic and paid labour, or find their lives unrewarding and isolating as they are trapped in family roles, are viewed as psychiatrically disturbed. There is a saying 'do not adjust your mind, there is a fault in reality', which could well be inscribed on the wall of every general practice waiting room.

The women's health movement is seeking more control for women over their health: control of their physical health, particularly as it relates to reproduction, and control of their mental health. The latter is particularly difficult, for as things stand women and their doctors rarely *do* have any immediate control over the social environment, from which so much mental ill-health stems. This is not to say that nothing can be done. Among its recommendations the Black Working Party called for adequate day-care for the under fives. High unemployment among women has not made this recommendation less important, as the government would have us believe. Quite the reverse. Proper childcare facilities are a vital provision for the health of children, their parents and the relationship between the two.

Providing women with more control by transforming their social environment clearly demands revolutionary changes which fall well outside the present remit of the NHS. Part of the fight for health is the fight for these changes. But more immediately the NHS could provide, for example, a network of well woman's clinics. The handbook for a trade union course on *Women and Health* in Manchester outlined the benefits:

> The idea of a well woman clinic is to have a place which is part of the National Health Service where women can go and discuss their health problems with women doctors and other women health workers. It is also somewhere from which women would be able to develop active community-based health education and preventive work extending out from the clinic building into the local area.

In close conjunction with well woman's clinics, women's support groups could be provided around general practices where the symptoms of isolation and stress present themselves, focusing attention onto a collective and social approach to women's health.

The women's movement is thus, on the one hand, calling for the provision of extended services for women under their own control. But it is also calling for changes in the medical view of women. The medical view of women, its implicit and explicit sexism, have been discussed by Lesley Doyal in *The Political Economy of Health*:

> Two basic ideas seem to be central to contemporary medical definitions of women. The first is the tacit belief that men are 'normal' whereas women are 'abnormal'. That is to say, the intellectual, emotional and physical potential of women is measured against the male standard and women are found to be

essentially defective. Secondly, this 'abnormality' is seen to de-
rive from the fact that the 'natural' role of women is to reproduce
and that this is the central determining characteristic of a
woman's being. The capacity to be a mother is no longer seen to
make women physically ill—just intellectually and emotionally
different and—by implication—inferior.
To change this view demands deep-seated changes in the way medicine is taught and in the content of the medical curriculum.

Alternative modes of treatment

Alternative therapies are varied. The British edition of *Our Bodies
Ourselves* by Angela Phillips and Jill Rakusen, includes a short
section outlining those most extensively employed. Other books,
such as *Fringe Medicine* by B. Inglis, include more detail.

Acupuncture is probably the best known of these therapies. It was
practised in China well over 2,000 years ago. It is still widely in use
there, often in conjunction with modern western medicines. Like
other alternative therapies, it is based upon the notion that the
human body has extensive powers of self-regulation. These can be
diminished by unhealthy influences from outside, bad nutrition, poor
breathing, lack of exercise or disease. And they can be assisted by
stimulating 'life energy pathways' by use of acupuncture needles
inserted at the right point.

Acupuncture is often used as a form of anaesthetic. The patient is
fully awake but has no sensation of a particular part of the body.
Operations performed under acupuncture embody a very different
relationship between the doctor performing the operation and the
patient. The patient enters hospital several days before the operation
to get to know the doctor and the other people involved, so that they
themselves become part of the 'team'.

The body's self-regulatory powers are exploited by other forms of
alternative medicine. The basis of homeopathy is to stimulate the
body's process of immunity by matching the signs and symptoms of
the patient with the substances which would most accurately reproduce those symptoms in a healthy person. A course of homeopathic
treatment involves in-depth study of the patient's life-style and eating
habits. Homeopathic treatment is one form of alternative therapy
that is available under the NHS, though doctors practising it will also
have to have undergone a traditional medical course. Angela Phillips
and Jill Rakusen made the important observation that 'the NHS

provides a further disincentive, as the payment per patient system discriminates against those who take more time with patients.'

Osteopathy, herbal medicines, naturopathy are all forms of treatment which *may* have much to offer the National Health Service in terms of therapy. Their effectiveness has not been properly tested; but then, as we have seen, neither have most conventional treatments. It is not, however, specific alternative remedies that I would advocate here. It would be as wrong to wheel on alternative medicines as means of treating the ills of capitalism as to wheel on the conventional. It is the *approach* embodied in these therapies from which we have most to learn.

Treatment of the whole body, rather than just the parts, focuses attention towards the environment of the person; not just eating and smoking habits and matters of personal life-style but occupation, housing and the other aspects of the life circumstances and life chances. And, as has been argued, recognition of the social dimension of ill health is recognition of the need for social action on ill-health.

Alternative medicines, as individual therapies, *can* be highly individualistic. Many now practising them would have very little in common with the aims of socialism. Their practice is often a part of the private sector that feeds off the National Health Service. But, distinguishing their progressive potential from their often regressive practice, they have much to offer from which the NHS could gain.

Summary

We have considered, in this chapter, ways that socialists can help the National Health Service to take a qualitative leap forward. By broadening the focus and extending the range of services available under the NHS we can both challenge and change its current direction. However, as we have seen, the current state of the NHS, and the health care it provides, are no historical accident. They are the product of the combination of forces that control it. To challenge the content is to challenge this control. It is therefore to the question of control that we now logically turn. How can the decision-making structure of the National Health Service be changed so that socialist items of health care provision can be placed firmly on the agenda?

6.

Opening Up Decision-Making in the Health Services

It has always seemed to me more than a little paradoxical that what can claim, in many respects, to be the most advanced socialist institution in British society is also one of the most undemocratic. If I am concerned about the education of my children, the efficiency of the transport system, the state of housing, either at a very particular level, or at a general level, there does exist, via the channels of local government, a machinery of decision-making which, nominally at least, allows me to raise my concerns with somebody who holds an elected position of statutory responsibility. If I am unhappy with a response that I get from the local head teacher, I can see my local councillor, who may raise the matter with the education committee or individually with its chairperson. If I am still unhappy, or it is a matter of general concern, I may approach the education system at a national level via my MP.

I am not saying that this system works particularly well, nor that in practice it affords democratic control. Individuals' complaints are not handled particularly responsively; only the articulate and confident will know how to approach the system; it is far too easy to get lost or fobbed off in the channels of bureaucracy. But at least the formal structure exists. Anyone who has ever tried to pursue an individual complaint against any part of or raise a general issue concerning the direction of the National Health Service will know that it's like trying to punch a jelly. As soon as you think you've hit it, it's gone.

The formal decision-making machinery of the NHS is constructed on the assumption that issues of health care delivery are non-political issues. This assumption constitutes the single most important failing of the original design of the NHS, and is directly responsible for a host of more minor failings. There *is* an official decision-making structure: the Department of Health and Social Security, regional health authorities and district health authorities. But the composition of the various tiers makes no pretence of democracy—they are all consitutued primarily from above; their formal powers are more supervisory than directive; and the individual membership is such as to guarantee virtual impotence. How can a district health authority, such as the new Sheffield District Health Authority, which is comprised of 19 local dignataries, most of whom are extremely busy and committed to other things, come together for just one afternoon every month and seriously hope to direct the health care for a population of over 500,000 people; supervising the operation of two district general hospitals, a number of smaller specialist hospitals and annexes, a host of general practitioner services, etc. *and* conduct broader discussion into the bargain?

This formal decision-making machinery is a blind, behind which an array of other bodies, individuals and organisations actually take decisions within the NHS. We have already identified most of these. Some are outside the National Health Service: the drug companies, the medical supply industry, the profiteers of the private medical sector. Others are within the NHS: individual powerful consultants or administrators. If we are to challenge seriously the direction of the National Health Service, a pre-condition must be to challenge the existing decision-making structure. We *must* establish a system which is controlled by and responsive to the needs of the people who use and work in the service. Without this, there can be no chance of our seeing the health service as an integral part of the movement towards a more compassionate society.

Reclaiming the National Health Service

We looked in chapter three at three areas where private companies currently enjoy rich pickings at the expense of the National Health Service. The point was stressed that such an arrangement is not only opposed to the socialist ideal of the NHS—that the delivery of good health care should be freed from the selfish laws of the capitalist market place— but it also provides a very severe constraint against a radical redirection of the health services.

Private capital's major interest in the health service is in the high-technology, acute sector. (Not that it isn't finding ways of 'making capital' from the middle classes' new-found concern for individual prevention). The medical supply industry is, obviously, concerned that the health service should continually be employing more, and more expensive, diagnostic and treatment gadgetry. A programme which seriously tackled the root cause of working women's ill-health, providing proper childcare and support services, could greatly reduce the vast profits from Valium and Librium overnight. A properly funded and structured approach to occupational and community health would take away the electricians' union's belief that they have anything to gain from negotiating a package of private care as part of a wage deal.

Private capital can promote its interest in medical care aggressively and effectively. Sometimes subtly, sometimes crudely, promotion and advertising can be very potent influences on the view of health care that exists within and around the health services. 'Toys for the boys' can look far more appealing and immediately productive than, say, campaigns on community health which will necessarily have longer term and probably less recognisable and immediately measurable effects.

One thing is sure. If private capital makes available and promotes a particular piece of technology, a particular drug or a particular private medical care facility, it will be in the interests of the profitability of private capital rather than the interests of good, equitable health care. This is not to say that there will never be benefits; but consideration of these will be coincidental.

Tighter control over the services and products currently provided to the health service by private industry will ensure that product development will be directed towards areas of *proven* effectiveness, and cost-effectiveness at that, having considered the potential value of alternative uses of the social investment. Will the investment in a new piece of technology have more value than the equivalent investment in a more labour-intensive community health development programme, when *all* dimensions of 'value' are considered, including, for example, current levels of unemployment? Products can be appraised similarly. Will the cost of distributing a particular drug be more worthwhile than the provision of an occupational health service in a particular place of work? These are not technical questions which can be 'scientifically' answered by avowedly non-political experts operating in 'either' private companies or public services. They are political issues, which can only be resolved by a process of political argument and debate. At the moment no political arena exists for their resolution. Nor could it until such issues are brought under the control of a genuinely democratic and fully informed decision-making process.

How can tighter control be effected? One element of the programme must be nationalisation. Nationalisation is the only mechanism by which more rational planning of product development can be ensured. As part of a comprehensive strategy of production for social need, drugs and new technology will be developed for the part they play in health promotion, rather than as part of private capital's short-term search for quick returns. Nationalisation will also ensure that any profit that accrues as the result of the distribution of these products, will be redirected in the interests of public health rather than private wealth.

The other element must be the elimination of private practice and private medicine. Improvements in the services provided under the NHS would severely reduce the general belief that the private sector offers a better quality of care. This can be coupled to a number of other strategies. The Fightback and Politics and Health Groups have argued against wholesale nationalisation of private medicine saying that 'It would saddle the NHS with the problem of running and financing expensive institutions providing the wrong kind of health care in the wrong part of the country—namely acute, high-technology services in and around London.' They have argued for the abolition of pay beds and for the use of nationalisation as a selective weapon. There is some merit in this strategy though we must guard against the danger identified earlier, of creating a two-tier service, which not only offends the ideal of a National Health Service, but also serves to move away from more basic community preventive programmes and the care of the long-stay non-chronically ill.

Democracy within the National Health Service

We looked very briefly in chapter four at the administrative structure that emerged from the 1974 reorganisation of the National Health Service: the complex bureaucracy with its (formerly three, now two) tiers of authority, composed of a peculiar mish-mash of members appointed from above, and a minority of local authority councillors. The philosophy behind the structure has been expressed as 'delegation downwards, accountability upwards'.

Real executive power lies with the district management team (DMT). The DMT consists of six people: administrator, finance officer, nursing officer, community physician, hospital consultant and GP (the last two elected by their colleagues)—see diagram 3. As the

Communist Party's evidence to the Royal Commission on the
National Health Service puts it, 'recommendations affecting two or
three thousand hospital beds come within the province of half-a-
dozen persons'. Once a month the district health authority, to which
the district management team is nominally accountable, meets to
consider an agenda of items which has normally been drawn up
between the chairperson of the district health authority and the
district management team.

Individual members of the authority do have the power to insert
items of business on the agenda. But how will they know what to put
on? They are largely reliant for their information on the district
management team. A few awkward questions may arise from the
monitoring that they conduct around the local health service facilities; but these visits can only be cosmetic in nature, rather than
substantial. Where the local authority is Labour controlled, a few
places on the authority are occupied by Labour councillors, who
might be expected to form the focal point of an 'opposition'. This is
rarely the case. Labour councillors from a controlling local authority
will fit the health authority in around their other commitments. In
Sheffield where, until the latest reorganisation of April 1982, a
'socialist group' of the local Labour councillors and other socialist
members actually constituted a majority on the old area health
authority, they were unable to effect any serious control over the
direction of services as the majority was normally eroded by bad
attendance. And, as we have seen nationally, the Labour Party's
commitment to a radical redirection of the National Health Service
has not been particularly marked.

The district management team plays a crucial role. It directs the
services and controls the information passing up to members of the
authority. The team's composition is medically dominated and it thus
has no serious interest in challenging the status quo of power and
control that exists on a day-to-day basis within the NHS. But do
authority members really need to be quite as impotent as, with the
best will in the world, they currently are?

There *are* other sources of information that authority members
could exploit—information that stems from the legitimate interests of
two groups who are now effectively excluded from the decision-
making processes. The two groups are the workers in the health
service and the users of the health service. Without their cumulative
knowledge the operation of the existing services cannot be monitored, let alone a serious reconsideration be mounted of the direction

of these services. In the short term information from these groups must be channelled into the existing decision-making machinery to 'dissident' members of authorities, so that the dominance of the district management team can be challenged. In the long term these groups must become part of the formal structure to counter the wider dominance of the medical profession.

Health service workers

Health service workers are represented by a patchwork of trade unions and professional organisations. The biggest health workers union is the National Union of Public Employees (NUPE) with approximately a quarter of a million members among manual workers from gardeners and domestic workers to porters and ambulance staff. The latter, in particular, and all manual workers in certain places, are sometimes organised by the Transport and General Workers Union (TGWU) and occasinally by the General and Municipal Workers Union (GMWU). In theory the industrial union for the NHS is the Confederation of Health Service Employees (COHSE). Previously as David Widgery points out, 'its real base' has been 'among the predominantly male mental hospitals', though in recent years this coverage has widened. Specialist workers have their own unions: laboratory staff, the Association of Scientific Technical and Managerial Staffs (ASTMS); construction workers, the Union of Construction, Allied Trades and Technicians (UCATT); and electricians, the Electrical, Electronic, Telecommunication and Plumbing Union (EETPU). Where unionised, administrative staff belong to the National and Local Government Officers Association, though its health service sections have something of a reputation for acting more as a staff association than a trade union. Nurses, who may belong to COHSE, may also belong to the professional organisation, the Royal College of Nursing (RCN). Like other professional organisations, the RCN tends to be dominated by its more senior members, though it was forced by its rank and file membership into adopting a militant campaign in the early 1970s and is now considering affiliation to the TUC. Doctors are organised, for want of a better word, by the British Medical Association, though ASTMS has a medical subsection, the Medical Practitioners Union, which recruited a number of members during the junior doctors dispute of 1975.

Apart from the medical profession, other workers have not expected nor have they sought to be involved in the decision-making processes of the National Health Service. They have tended to restrict their concern to traditional trade union matters of pay and working conditions. This is understandable; particularly at a time of recession and contractions, invitations to workers to 'participate' in the decision-making process are normally a ploy by management to hand over the decisions about where the cuts that they've already decided upon are to be implemented, thus heading off future worker resistance, on the grounds that they've already been consulted. But it is also unfortunate. Health service workers have a wealth of experience that is going to waste. It is the 'shop floor' workers of the service, the ambulance drivers, the nurses, the portering staff, who have the day-to-day contact with the patients and have the best general view of the operation of the services. It is, for example, the ambulance drivers going from home to home who see the effectiveness of community care and the adequacy or otherwise of the support services offered. They can tell you, as they have told me, of old people sitting in darkness because they are unable to change a light bulb, of old people sitting in the cold because they have been told that their central heating system needs bleeding, and have turned it off, thinking this made it dangerous. The collective experience of the workforce not only puts it in the best position to monitor, but is the best starting point from which to plan ahead.

The arrogance of the professional and managerial classes leads them to believe that they, and only they, because of their special background, training and skills, have acquired a god-given right to manage. Indeed, the only justification there can be for the additional power, money and status that accrue to people in controlling positions generally is the belief that they have a special right and power to manage which attracts these privileges.

The capitalist conception of management is individualistic and hierarchical, with the individual manager, or board, at the top of a pyramid. As owner of capital, or as agent for the owners of capital, management works from the top downwards, with the layers below carrying out their functions as directed. This view of management has been incorporated into the NHS since its inception, but was most specifically the model behind the restructuring of 1974.

The true socialist conception of management is different. It is collective and it is democratic. Individual managers, where they continue to exist, are not supremos, lords of all they survey, expected to order and control everything below them; they are the agents of the workforce and the users subject to direction from 'below', synthesising the maybe conflicting views, exploring consequences, and referring the actual decision-making back to the democratic process.

Where the workforce has been given, or rather has taken, the lead over matters of planning and direction it has been demonstrated clearly that vision and imagination are not somehow absorbed from the walls of public schools and universities but grow from hard practical day-to-day experience. The most ample source of such experience is, in industrial locations, the workforce and its shop floor representation in the shop stewards committee. The Lucas Aerospace Combine Committee found itself, in the late sixties, faced with the familiar prospect of job losses. But the circumstances of the Lucas workers were a little different. Lucas Aerospace is primarily a producer of weapons of war. To defend their jobs the shop stewards would, normally, have found themselves defending the greater proliferation of these weapons. Having undertaken a systematic audit of the skills and resources available within the workforce, the Combine Committee took the imaginative step of drawing up an alternative plan for the company. This plan included 150 different products, all of which were selected on criteria of social usefulness rather than capitalist profitability. They were products which could be produced then and there with the facilities available, and all of which related directly to social need.

Community involvement

The health services exist to cater for patients and potential patients in the community. For capitalist management, patients are an additional headache, another sector at the bottom of the pyramid to be directed, controlled, cajoled and generally contended with. For socialist management, patients are an additional resource, a complementary source of experience, vision and imagination, which can interact with that of the workforce, allowing each to expand and develop.

A number of progressive general practices have experimented with setting up patients' committees. Their functions and powers vary from practice to practice. But, at a general level, they exist to provide the practices with feedback from and a measure of control by the community. If these are to develop, as they should, they must have the power to really influence services rather than being merely 'talk shops'.

In setting up community health councils, the Conservative and

Labour governments did in the main succeed in their task of providing an outlet for community dissatisfaction—a drain through which discontent could be drawn off and allowed to trickle harmlessly away. Because of their composition, largely appointed rather than elected, they provide a glorious opportunity for local Jimmy Savilles to display vociferously their good works and concern for others, and in the process act as a barrier to public misgivings behind which the health service can be allowed to continue functioning as normal. For capitalist management, they were a way of taking care of that particularly awkward factor, the local community.

However, in creating the CHCs, the governments did also open up new possibilities. The chances were remote, given their structures, but the vision, energy and enthusiasm of a handful of individual CHC members and secretaries, some of whom have been sacked as a result, has developed for a few community health councils the same role in the local community as that filled by joint shop stewards committees in the workplace.

As with the Lucas shop stewards Combine Committee, it has normally been a position of defence which has been the catalyst for the flourishing of this imagination and vision. We have already seen when looking at the opposition movements that have grown up against cuts in the NHS how, in certain places, CHCs have become an important focal point. We have also seen, particularly in relation to the Elizabeth Garrett Anderson Hospital in London, though it has also happened elsewhere, how this originally defensive position has turned into a more aggressive, questioning stance, raising many of the concerns about the direction of the health service that have been summarised in the chapter above.

Jeannette Mitchell, former secretary of Brent Community Health Concil, made the connection between the fight for the creation of a community hospital out of the threatened Willesden General Hospital and the Lucas Combine Committee's fight, in a paper presented to a one-day workshop on workers' plans for health organised by the Centre for Alternative Industrial and Technological Systems:

> But also like industry, health services have the potential to meet people's needs. And the vast majority of people who work in and use hospitals have a much better idea of what should happen in them and how things could be organised than the people currently in control, who have different interests to serve. Fighting for a health service to meet our needs and fighting for socially useful work are a part of the same struggle.

Community and workers' plans

Socialists fighting for a broader based, more democratic and more equitable health service have much to gain, tactically and strategically, from conducting the fight from organisations based upon community and worker interest and involvement in health. Health service unions have been more reluctant than community groups to embark upon offensive campaigns. Community groups coming to trade unionists have often been irritated to find them backing off as campaigns extended beyond traditional union concerns of pay, conditions and, particularly, defence of jobs.

It is possible, although not necessarily the case, that the type of community-worker movement advocated here is most useful when the impetus can be created from within the labour movement. In Coventry, the trades council established a health sub-committee. In 1979, this sub-committee instituted a 'workers' enquiry into health'. As Hilary Barker and Mick Carpenter put it in a paper to the same workshop on workers' plans for health:

> In some ways the term 'workers enquiry' is a misnomer, it could imply a concern with workplace issues to the exclusion of family and community health. But it does signify our ties with the labour movement through the trades council . . . [The enquiry aims to adopt] a broad-fronted strategy and look at both issues of finance and the quality of health care in Coventry's health service.

In similar vein, we have, in Sheffield, recently established a socialist Health Care Strategy Group. This is a slightly more formally constituted group being comprised of socialist members of Sheffield District Health Authority, representatives of the Labour group and Labour Party, the trades council, the community health council, the Socialist Health Association, trade union lay members and officers, and members of four radical health groups. This is a fragile composition, bringing together people whose style of working is often very dissimilar and who are unaccustomed to working together. Initially it has been concerned with exploring the implications of the Black Report for Sheffield as a prelude to constructing a comprehensive socialist health strategy.

Such coalitions of interest groups are essential. Out of them we may form community and worker plans for the creation of a socially useful health service, directed towards the real health needs of the workers and users, rather than the needs of commercial and professional interests. A broadly based socialist health movement created out of the existing health groups and unions will not only provide a focus from which the current power structure can be challenged, opened-up and democratised, it will also be an important forerunner of the administration of health care and health services within a genuinely socialist society.

Summary

We have looked in this chapter at the various ways that decision-making within the National Health Service can be made more accountable. Firstly, it must be freed from the outside influences which control and distort the patterns of health care delivered. But also, it must be democratised internally, so that the interests of the workers and the users of the health service are given full say. These are preconditions for the establishment and existence of health care services under socialism, to which we finally turn.

7.

Health Care and Socialism

Models of socialism

The argument put forward in this book can be stated quite simply. It is possible to enact fragments of socialism within an economic and political framework that is essentially capitalist in nature. We have studied the National Health Service as an example of this general 'law'. With the best will in the world, it is not possible to establish a system of health care which is free at the time of use, freely accessible to all and meets everyone's health needs within the constraint of a capitalist economy. The fundamental dynamic of that society, which is to generate and accumulate capital, will consistently intrude, undermine and distort the egalitarian goal of a potentially socialist health care system.

The all-pervasive nature of the capitalist economic system is such that no fundamentally contradictory social experiment, such as a socialist health service, could coexist with it. The subtlety and sophistication of the modern capitalist system lies in its ability not to outlaw and forcibly remove such experiments but to systematically distort them so that they themselves become part of that capitalist system. We have tried to illustrate this process with respect to the NHS. What was, 35 years ago, a beacon to socialism, has become another arena within which privately, or if need be, publicly owned capital can accumulate. And, as we saw in chapter three, it can be a highly profitable arena at that. It is largely the labour movement's fault if that beacon has dimmed. In the cosy years of the 1950s and 1960s it allowed itself to be lulled into the belief that a humane form of capitalism, liberal social democracy, might be able to fulfill the promises that had previously been held out solely by socialism. The 1970s have shown and the 1980s will undoubtedly continue to show this to be an illusion. When the capitalist economy hits rough water, as it must from time to time as part of its continuing process of rejuvenation, it is the social welfare provisions, just those socialist experiments, that will be jettisoned to lighten the capitalist ship.

The only possibilities for the development and expansion of such social reforms, which must be the foundation stones for a compassionate and caring society, are to see them not as appendages which can be pinned to a fundamentally inhumane system in an attempt to humanise it, but part of the continuing, developing and expanding process of creating a socialist society. It is tempting, and it would perhaps be easiest and safest, to end this book there—with a simple assertion of the need to re-invigorate the struggle for socialism with the defence of the initial aspirations of the NHS as part of that struggle. However, history has taught us not only about the dynamics of capitalism but also the dynamics of emerging socialism. It is not enough simply to assert that things will somehow come right 'after the revolution'. Revolutions have happened, peaceful ones and violent ones, and things have often gone very wrong. There is not space to consider here how things did go wrong after, for example, the Russian revolution. Suffice it to say that Russian society currently stands as far removed from a genuinely socialist society as most of the western liberal capitalist societies, notwithstanding the many highly developed aspects of its welfare and social structure. We need a clear vision of the society that we are constructing in order to avoid repeating the errors of the past.

We also need a clear vision of the society that we are constructing because we can not guarantee that the process will be an easy one. It will undoubtedly demand some hardships and almost certainly some sacrifices. The lessons of Chile are clearest: where 'autonomous' nations try to negotiate their way peaceably and democratically towards a socialist society imperialist nations such as the United States of America feel that they *must* interfere and subvert that democratic process. Things are not normally allowed to go as far as they did in Chile, the process can normally be subverted at a much earlier stage. But serious attempts to break out of the shackles of *either* of the major imperialist powers, be they in Poland or in El Salvador, or indeed should they be in Britain, will meet with the resistance of whichever power views that territory as belonging within its 'sphere of influence'. Moves to a genuinely socialist society would be seen by either as inimicable to its long term interests and would be resisted, initially by underhand subversion but, if need be, by outright force.

Unless we have some idea of where we are going it will be very hard to convince others, or indeed possibly ourselves, that it's all going to be worth it.

Constructing models of post-capitalist society has normally been the reserve of 'utopian socialists' and anarchists. Mainstream socialism has shied away from the highly speculative activity of offering visions of the future. In some respects it has been right. Socialist societies will be moulded in the process of their creation. The liberated democracy that will be the essence of these societies will open up a richness and wealth of possibilities that can only be dimly made out from the confines and constraints of the world imposed upon all of us by the society we now inhabit. It would be arrogant to claim otherwise. We can, however, with confidence lay down some of the broad characteristics which must be absolute pre-conditions of socialist society. It must be non-sexist, non-racist and non-hierarchical. We can, in part, define the outlines of that society in negative terms, asserting characteristics which are fundamentally incompatible with socialism. A society which allows privileged access to, or control over its resources by an individual member or group within that society by virtue of sex, race *or* position is denying the free democracy upon which socialism must be founded.

Can we move from negative characteristics to positive characteristics? Percival and Paul Goodman in their classic and futuristic study of planning, *Communitas*, published in New York, offer three 'community paradigms'. 'We present three alternative models of choices with regard to technology, surplus, and the relation of means and ends, and we ask what each formula gives us in economics, politics, education, domestic standards, popular and high culture, and other functions of the community.' Of the three schemes that they develop they express their own preference for the second, which starts from the elimination of difference between production and consumption, but their preferences are hardly the point. The point of such 'utopian' exercises, which are too complex to consider in depth here, is to demonstrate two aspects of post-capitalist societies. They must embody a pluralism and they will reflect in their organisation fundamental questions about human relations and the relationship of the human species to the rest of the 'natural' world.

The two are closely related. The richness and variety of people's abilities, skills, interests and experiences lead them to wish for differing social relations and differing relations with the natural world. Some will wish to form larger communities, some smaller communi-

ties. Some will wish to employ higher technology, in full awareness of
its implications for themselves and others; some will wish to live in
closer relationship with the natural environment. All possibilities
should be realisable, so long as the cardinal tenet is acknowledged
that one group's choices should in no way inhibit or exploit the
choices of others, then or in the future. This will demand a variety of
organisations, freely entered into and coming together to resolve
matters of mutual interest and concern.

Each will embody different social and environmental relations.
The oppressive reality of advanced industrial capitalist societies is
that they embody underlying social values and choices which few are
able to challenge and from which it is impossible to free yourself.
Most significant of these is the primacy of the production process and
the position of the different classes in relation to it. Anna Coote, in
an article in the November/December 1981 edition of *New Socialist*,
in which she criticises the emphasis on production and the relations
between labour and capital in the Alternative Economic Strategy,
raises the following possibility: 'Rather than asking in the first instance: "how can we regenerate industry in order to create full employment?", we might begin with a different kind of question, such as
"how shall we care for and support our children?".' There are a
range of such questions, the answers to which have profound implications for family relations, the organisation of domestic work, the
primacy of the reproductive role, the organisation of childcare, and
our exploitation of natural resources. They will not only determine
the short-term strategy which we employ to combat the capitalist
economic system—the context in which Anna Coote raised them—
but also the society, or more accurately range of societies, which will
emerge from that struggle and which must be prefigured in the course
of it. Not least of these questions will be those that relate to issues of
health, ill-health and the manner in which we choose to deliver health
care and health services.

The socialist view of health

We will return to the more detailed questions of health care and
health services a little later on. But before we can start to consider
them we must first consider what we mean by 'health'.

The socialist view of health is reflected in the perhaps unexpected
setting of the Constitution of the World Health Organisation:

Health is a state of complete physical, mental, and social well-being, and not merely the absence of disease or infirmity. The enjoyment of the highest attainable standard of health is one of the fundamental rights of every human being, without distinction of race, religion, political beliefs, economic and social conditions. The health of all peoples is fundamental to the attainment of peace and security, and is dependent upon the fullest co-operation of the individuals and states . . . Health development of the child is of basic importance; the ability to live harmoniously in a changed total environment is essential to such development . . .

Governments have a responsibility for the health of their peoples, which can be fulfilled only by their provision of adequate health and social measures.

These passages illustrate two of the basic assumptions behind a socialist view of health. The first is that health must be viewed not simply as the individual's concern but as a social concern. Health problems are social problems. We have discussed this particular limitation of the capitalist view of health and ill-health already and need not dwell on it here. The second basic assumption is the one directly stated in the first sentence, that health is more than just the absence of disease or infirmity, being a state of positive well-being.

This positive concept of health existed long before the socialist movement as we know it. It existed before capitalism, in the context of which modern socialist ideas have evolved. M. Wilson, in *Health is for the People*, discusses the Navaho conception of health, as a state symptomatic of a correct relationship between man, or woman, and his/her environment, including other men and women. Wilson draws the two assumptions together in saying that: 'health is a word related to the quality of human life in ecological terms, that is, not just an individual quality, but is related to life lived together in harmony with the environment.' Capitalism has replaced this view of health as social well-being with one of health as merely the opposite to disease. If you are not in need of treatment, in that you have identifiable curable symptoms of physical or psychological maladjustment, then you are not ill and must, therefore, be in a state of health.

The socialist view of health must re-capture the conception of health as positive well-being. A necessary condition for this well-being is a conducive social environment. Thus, health matters and other social matters cannot be viewed as separable but part of a continuous ecological balance. Similarly, the individual person will not be seen as divisable, to be broken down into a kit of parts each of which can be treated in isolation. The socialist view of health is holistic, with regard both to the individual and to society. The individual is viewed as a whole person and an integral part of a whole society. Problems of maladjustment *may* be perceived at an individual level, in a particular disease or an accident, but they will, at the same time, be problems for the whole society. Thus, to quote again from M. Wilson: 'Health is the milieu (human and environmental) which enables people individually and socially to grow towards fullness of life.'

Socialist health care

The socialist conception of health can be seen in part translated into health care and health services in a number of countries which are struggling to move beyond capitalism. In particular, much has been written about and learnt from health care in Cuba and Mozambique, both trying to combine a system of health care delivery which is a signpost to the socialist future with one which is most effective in dealing with the legacy of a colonial past. Even countries in the eastern bloc, the Soviet Union and the German Democratic Republic, despite their other shortcomings, provide some ideas for health services, such as their occupational health services, from which we have much to learn. But probably most advanced, in terms of offering a picture of health care which is neither immediately concerned with rectifying a colonial past nor coupled to a highly technological view of the future and which is informed by many centuries tradition of holistic medicine is China.

It is not suggested that any of the health systems of the countries mentioned here offer precise models which we might see duplicated in a future socialist Britain. Circumstances, historical, cultural and geographical, are very different. And it is these that will determine the exact details of British socialism and the nature of health care within a socialist Britain. We can however extract some general principles from the experiences of health care in Cuba, Mozambique and China, each of which, as socialist principles, are closely interrelated and might be expected to underpin any socialist health care system.

In accord with the expanded concept of health, each of these countries views the provision of health care as much more than simply the organisation of health services. A report on 'Health care in Cuba', reprinted in *Medicine in Society*, illustrates this 'new

approach to health' (if not an awareness of the perpetuation of sex
roles through language):

> The basic concept of health which guides the development of
> Cuba's health care program is a very broad one. It consists of a
> manifold of factors, woven into the fabric of a person's life—his
> work, his living conditions, his social environment, his personal
> fulfillment. In socialist Cuba, health care is an integral part of the
> entire process of economic and social planning. Housing de-
> velopments are never built without a polyclinic, factories are
> constructed with medical facilities and safety measures incorpo-
> rated in the blueprint; schools are run with the understanding
> that good health is indispensable for effective learning.

Cuba is a society in which the road to socialism is closely linked to the
process of industrialisation. Thus there is still a hint, in the quotation
above, that health planning is something that follows in the wake of
economic planning. However, what is clear is that health care is seen
as an important component, one might say 'cost', of the industrialisation process, the health consequences of which are to be minimised.
This can be contrasted with present day Britain, where health care is
seen as something that must come *after* the process of industrial
recovery since, we are told, we cannot now afford it—despite the
quantity of health care resources and potential resources currently
lying idle.

At a personal level this 'new approach to health' is reflected in the
provision of health care by health teams. These are particularly
important for primary health care in both Cuba and Mozambique.
With their additional years of experience, years which have enabled
them to correct most of the unhealthy legacy of colonialism and to
develop their own particular style of health care, the Cubans have
developed this team approach particularly well. One interesting feature of the Cuban health teams is that together with more traditional
medical staff (the general doctor, obstetrician/gynaecologist,
paediatrician, nurse and doctor) and the social support staff (psycho-
logist, social worker, sanitary worker and physical therapist) the
teams also include a statistician, reflecting an awareness that monitoring is an extremely important component of good basic health care.

In China, with its vast rural populations, the various functions of
the health team are often combined into a single person—the cele-
brated 'barefoot doctor'. As is clear from the experiences related by
one English doctor, Joshua Horn, in his autobiographical account of
life as a health worker in China, the tasks of the barefoot doctor go

well beyond the conventional province of the medic. The same model of decentralised health care has been seen as appropriate for the more inaccessible areas of Mozambique, which cannot be immediately serviced by a full team. Malcolm Segall writes of his own experiences in Mozambique: 'Acting as a link between the health centre and the organised village population, they [the Mozambican equivalent of the Chinese barefoot doctor] will be involved mainly in mobilising people for their own health promotion, whilst also providing simple treatments.' He goes on to explain, 'They are chosen by the villages from amongst their members with at least four years primary schooling', reflecting another important aspect of socialist health care, that it revolves less around the highly professional image of the doctor. This was, of course, in Mozambique and in Cuba, a principle born somewhat out of necessity, as they both lost the bulk of their highly trained medical staff who sought to retain their privileged status by fleeing to countries where medical staff are rewarded in more material ways. But it is a principle which is deeply enshrined in the socialist concept of health care.

Together with this de-professionalisation of health care has come a democratisation of its control. In Cuba, the local mass organisations, the Committees for the Defence of the Revolution and the Federation of Cuban Women, play a very important, active part in mounting health campaigns, running clinics, and not least co-operating in the data collection and screening. They are not just more democratic yet equally remote 'bosses' passively directing the services. In Mozambique, the villages from which they are chosen are expected to guarantee the food and shelter of their health worker and to build a small health post using local materials. Thus, health care is not something which is anonymously imposed from above, but something to which everybody contributes and directs.

Socialist health services

In all these emerging socialist countries the most striking feature has been the new importance ascribed to primary health care services. This has by no means been purely an ideological choice, reflecting the increased democratic control and involvement that can be effected with respect to primary care. It has been also of the greatest practical importance. The story of success in Cuba has been remarkable. Within the 20 years after 1959, and despite the very severe setbacks that followed the post-revolutionary medical exodus, fatalities from typhoid, diphtheria, polio and malaria were eliminated and mortality from tuberculosis reduced dramatically. Life expectancy now stands on a par with European countries. This has been achieved by the widespread extension of primary care and preventive programmes, but not at the neglect of secondary services.

Prior to 1959, Cuban hospital beds were provided almost exclusively in the urban centres. A programme of building rural hospitals, together with an improved transportation system has brought secondary care within easy access of even the most outlying rural areas. Again, this must be contrasted with the British system where closure of cottage hospitals has pushed secondary care back onto large district general hospitals almost exclusively concentrated in the major conurbations

It should be stressed that socialism is not just a matter of seeking improved secondary care facilities, but secondary care facilities which embody a different relationship between patient and health specialist. It is, for example, seemingly paradoxical that at a time when large numbers of women in Britain are fighting for the right to have their children at home, Cuba boasts that 95 per cent of all births are now taking place in hospitals. The paradox is only superficial. Women in Britain are reacting against the dehumanised 'care' that they receive in hospitals, with its undue use of interventionist technology, employed to induce childbirth, for example, at the convenience of the medical staff. Very few would reject the availability of the medical equipment that is on hand in hospitals, and its use if necessary for the health of their child or their own health. Dehumanised treatment and medical technology need not go hand in hand.

We could provide 'technology with a human face' not only for childbirth but as a general principle for all forms of secondary medical care. The different relationship between health team and patient which exists in the Chinese health system was commented upon when we briefly discussed acupuncture. This team approach which includes the patient as the most important member, can provide the patient with the opportunity to participate in a fully-informed decision concerning the course of treatment that is in his or her own best interest. This is rarely a purely clinical decision. But even where it is there is absolutely no reason why the specialist should not act as 'interpreter' to provide the patient with the necessary knowledge. The very word 'patient' is loaded, implying passiveness. We might expect to see it replaced by a more active term such as 'user'. First though, medical specialists need to develop skills in personal relations and communications which are positively excluded by the elitist training of the British medical profession.

How to control technology is a problem which must be confronted in many areas of a socialist society, not just the health services. Capitalist society produces capitalist technology constructed from a capitalist science by capitalist relations of production. Under socialism, things will be different all along the line. The enthusiasm with which the Lucas Aerospace workers leapt to turn their knowledge and skills to socially useful production, which included (not without criticism) items of medical equipment, should allay any fears that modern technology is inextricably linked to alienated labour. People like to be creative. It is a rewarding experience to see the finished product of your own, individual or collective, labour. It is even more rewarding if that product can be put to serve the needs of other people. Decisions about socialist medical technology will be made in full awareness of the conditions of their production. Again, as Paul and Percival Goodman have demonstrated, there are a number of quite distinct ways of resolving the various choices concerning the production and use of technology, each of which will reflect underlying values. Each should be available to a future socialist society, even if some will necessarily be rejected.

Summary

In the latter part of this chapter we have tended to draw at some length on the experienes of other societies at their various stages in the development of a fully fledged socialist society. These experiences are offered as examples of the possible rather than as models to be copied. The point has been made that the road to socialism in Britain will, in many ways, be a specifically British road, informed by British culture, environment and experience.

It will be from these characteristics that some of the very important issues, such as the relationship of professionals, particularly those in the health field, to other members of society, and the society's employment and control of technology, will come to be resolved. There will of course be many others, such as the experience of and preparation for death, that will occupy socialist caring services, and that we haven't considered at all here.

It is very unsatisfactory to close a book on loose ends. But this is to some extent inevitable when the discussion moves from a consideration of capitalism to a consideration of socialism. To recall the earlier points, I endeavoured to show how a large portion of the illness and disease that we currently experience in British society stems from its political and economic organisation as a capitalist society. Furthermore, I argued that sections within that society are currently making very substantial profits out of that illness and disease. I went on the consider the consequences of these, and other aspects of its capitalist location, for the British National Health Service. I then suggested ways in which that service could be broadened and made more democratic in order that it might realise some of the socialist potential that has lain dormant since its foundation.

This potential is probably the most fitting conclusion to this book. The British National Health Service is a monument to the possible. It is an example which other countries struggling to free themselves from the constraints of earlier backward regimes have done well to try to learn from. But it is also a monument to the practical. The practical limitations of what can be achieved within the framework of a capitalist society. The National Health Service is an important achievement which has still to realise a fraction of its real potential. The argument for a comprehensive health service, free at the time of use, is as valid now as it was 40 years ago. We have extended it to assert also the need for equally distributed 'health chances'. It is this argument which is the argument for socialism.

A Guide to Reading

Place of publication is London unless otherwise indicated.

Chapter 1.

Details of the structure of the health services that preceded the NHS can be found in D. Stark Murray, *The Future of Medicine*, Penguin Special 1942. For a wealth of reminiscences dating from an earlier period, see Margaret Llewelyn Davies (ed.), *Maternity: Letters from Working Women*, Virago 1978.

Chapter 2.

The evidence of the persistent social class inequalities in ill-health and the usage and availability of the health services has been collected together by the Black Working Party in its report, *Inequalities in Health: Report of a Research Working Group*, DHSS 1980. A similar collation for child health has been completed in M. Blaxter, *The Health of the Children*, Heinemann 1981. Both of these compilations relied upon a number of sources, the most substantial of which is the decennial supplement, Office of Population Censuses and Surveys, *Occupational Mortality, 1970–1972*, HMSO 1978.

That these inequalities have their origins in the different classes' experience of the consequences of a capitalist organisation of society has been argued forcibly and thoroughly in L. Doyal, *The Political Economy of Health*, Pluto Press 1979, and Sheffield SHA branch, *National Health and Social Sickness*, Socialist Health Association 1982, and implicitly in I. Gibson, *Class Health and Profit*, Norwich: University of East Anglia 1981 and Unit for the Study of Health

Policy, *Health Money and the National Health Service*, Guy's Hospital Medical School 1976.

Reviews of the specific fields in which the classes experience the ill-health consequences of a capitalist society can be found, amongst other places, in the World Health Organisation, *Health Hazards of the Human Environment*, Geneva: WHO 1972. Though for a comprehensive review of each area it is necessary to turn to the more specialist publications.

For the ill-health consequences of different areas of employment P. Kinnersley, *The Hazards of Work*, Pluto Press 1973, offers a comprehensive guide. This is updated regularly by the British Society for Social Responsibility in Science's (BSSRS) Work Hazards Group in its bi-monthly *Hazards Bulletin* and in its specialist pamphlets series which has now included the following titles: *Noise*; *Oil*; *Vibration*; *Asbestos*; and the *Office Workers Survival Handbook*. (BSSRS can be contacted at 9 Poland Street, London W1V 3DG). The Leeds busworkers enquiry was reported in *Stress at Work: Final Report*, Leeds: T&GWU 9/12 branch March 1981.

The earlier work on unemployment and health was reported in S. V. Kasl, S. Cobb and S. Gore, 'Changes in reported illness and illness behaviour related to termination of employment: a preliminary report', *International Journal of Epidemiology*, vol. 1 no. 2, 1972, pp. 111–118. Discussion on the subject was recently revived by two reports from Harvey Brenner: M. H. Brenner, *Estimating the Social Costs of National Economic Policy*, Washington: US Government Printing Office 1976, and M. H. Brenner, 'Mortality and the national economy', *The Lancet*, 15 September 1979, pp. 568–573, which have produced considerable argument reviewed in 'The big debate: Does the recession kill?', *Times Health Supplement*, 30 October 1981, pp. 14–15.

The influence of housing on health has proved a difficult area on which to compile evidence, as mentioned in the main body of the text. A specific study which has proved more informative has been that of D. M. Wilner and others, *The Housing Environment and Family Life*, Baltimore: Johns Hopkins Press 1962. A consideration of different areas can be found in L. E. Hinkle and W. C. Loring (eds.), *The Effects of the Man-made Environment on Health and Behaviour*, Castle House Publications 1979, and shorter reviews in M. Brennan and V. Little, 'Housing and health', *Medicine in Society*, vol. 5 no. 4, 1979, pp. 8–11; and C. Bedale and T. Fletcher, 'A damp site worse', *Times Health Supplement*, 12 February 1982, p.

15. For a specific example of a study showing the statistical relationship between housing and ill-health, see M. E. Brennan and R. Lancashire, 'Association of childhood mortality with housing status and unemployment', *Journal of Epidemiology and Community Health*, vol. 32, 1978, pp. 28–33. For a study on overcrowding and health, see A. Booth and J. Cowell, 'Crowding and health', *Journal of Health and Social Behaviour*, vol. 17, 1976, pp. 204–220. And for a study illustating the problems of separating out housing history see J. W. G. Yarnell and A. St Leger, 'Housing conditions, respiratory illness, and lung function in children in South Wales', *British Journal of Preventive and Social Medicine*, vol. 31, 1977, pp. 183–188.

The relationship of nutrition to health has been considered in the Politics of Health Group's pamphlet *Food and Profit*, PoHG 1979 (PoHG can be contacted via the British Society for Social Responsibility in Science), and the BSSRS's Agricapital Group's bulletin *Food and Politics*. Detailed consideration of specific diseases known to be related to the western diet are to be found in D. P. Burkitt and M. C. Trowell (eds.), *Refined Carbohydrate Foods and Disease*, London: Academic Press 1975. See also Sir Richard Doll, 'Strategy for detection of cancer hazards to man', *Nature*, vol. 265, 17 February 1977, pp. 589–596.

Little has been written on the general relationship between private transport and health, though it is frequently touched on in the publictions of the Unit for the Study of Health Policy. A comprehensive review of the specific consequences of accidents is contained in 'Speed kills', *Times Health Supplement*, 11 December 1981, pp. 12–13.

There is substantial information now available on the effect of air pollution on health, although most of it can only be traced by scouring the specialist journals. A thorough review of this area is given by J. R. Goldsmith and L. T. Friberg, 'Effects of air pollution on human health', in A. C. Stern (ed.), *Air Pollution Vol. II—The Effects of Air Pollution*, Academic Press 1977, chapter 7. Generally considered to be disappointing was a DHSS working party's report on lead in the environment, *Lead and Health*, HMSO 1980, though it contains a full review of studies of the neuropsychological effects of lead on children.

Evidence on the ill-health experiences of ethnic minorities is reviewed in M. Grimsley, S. Nicholas and C. Thunhurst, 'Health and social services', in Runnymede Trust and the Radical Statistics Race Group, *Britain's Black Population*, Heinemann 1980, chapter 6.

Illustrative accounts of black people's experiences of the health services are given in *Black People and the Health Service*, Brent Community Health Council 1981. And necessary measures to effect remedial action are proposed in *Health Link*, the quarterly newsletter of the Community Health Group for Ethnic Minorities.

The women's movement has spawned considerable material on women's health, the most comprehensive of which remains the Boston Women's Health Book Collective, *Our Bodies Ourselves*, British edition by A. Phillips and J. Rakusen, Penguin 1978. L. Doyal, *The Political Economy of Health*, Pluto Press 1979, integrates a feminist perspective on health and health services with a general socialist perspective and the *Office Workers' Survival Handbook*, BSSRS Publications 1981, identifies hazards of work predominantly faced by women. The work of George W. Brown and his co-researchers on schizophrenia and depression in women is briefly reviewed in G. W. Brown 'Social causes of disease', in D. Tuckett (ed.), *An Introduction to Medical Sociology*, Tavistock 1976.

Chapter 3.

D. Widgery, *Health in Danger*, Macmillan 1979, contains two chapters, 6 and 7 respectively, in which he offers a very readable account of the effects of the drug industry and private practice on the National Health Service, as does the Counter Information Services report, *NHS—Condition Critical*, CIS 1981.

A number of pamphlets have been written on the effects of private practice on the NHS most recent of which are Fightback/Politics of Health Group, *Going Private*, PoHG/Fightback 1981 and S. Iliffe, *Conditional Critical*, Communist Party of Great Britain 1982. The Radical Statistics Health Group in its pamphlet *In Defence of the NHS*, RSHG 1977, discuss the effects of private medicine in the context of other recent attacks on the NHS, such as the move for greater insurance funding.

The practices of the drugs industry and their relationship to the health services are discussed in Alan Klass, *There's Gold in Them Thar Pills*, Penguin 1975. The discussion is set in the context of the British NHS in J. Robson, *Take a Pill . . .* , Marxists in Medicine 1972, and the Labour Party, *The Pharmaceutical Industry*, Labour Party 1976 and in an international context, particularly as it relates to the Third World, in the Haslemere Group, *Who Needs the Drug Companies?*, Haslemere Group 1975; T. Heller, *Poor Health, Rich*

Profits, Nottingham: Spokesman 1977; and C. Medawar, *Insult or Injury?*, Social Audit 1979, which also considers the marketing and advertising of British food in the Third World.

Less attention has been paid to the medical supply industry, though B. Stocking and S. L. Morrison, *The Image and the Reality*, Oxford: Nuffield Provincial Hospitals Trust 1978, offers a well researched account of the development of computerised tomography scanners as a case-study of the impacts of medical technology, and the *Times Health Supplement* has recently carried a number of informative articles in its occasional series, Hi-Tech.

Chapter 4.

Again, D. Widgery, *Health in Danger*, Macmillan 1979 includes chapters on the development of the British National Health Service in the context of British capitalism, paying particular attention to the period of 'the cuts'. A view of the National Health Service as being almost exclusively 'functional' to the development of British capitalism is given in V. Navarro, *Class Struggle, The State and Medicine*, Martin Robertson 1978.

Accounts of the birth of the National Health Service are given by D. Stark Murray, *Why a National Health Service*, Pemberton Books 1971, which concentrates on the role of the Socialist Medical Association; H. Eckstein, *The English Health Service*, Cambridge: Harvard University Press 1959; and J. E. Pater, *The Making of the National Health Service*, King Edward's Hospital Fund 1981.

A large number of pamphlets have been produced in opposition to the recent programme of cuts in the NHS. Those placed in a more general context have been the Politics of Health Group, *Cuts and the NHS*, PoHG; and Counter Information Services, *NHS—Condition Critical*, CIS 1981. Illustrative of those that have concentrated on local struggles have been J. Salvage and K. Boomla, *The NHS in East London. What Lies Ahead?*, Keep Bethnal Green Hospital Campaign; and Sheffield Campaign Against the Cuts in the Health Services, *Towards a Socialist Health Service*, Sheffield 1979.

The health care delivered within the NHS has been explored particularly by the women's movement in, for example, L. Doyal, *The Political Economy of Health*, Pluto Press 1979, and Boston Women's Health Book Collective, *Our Bodies Ourselves*, Penguin 1978, and the various pamphlets of the Politics of Health Group. Critical evaluation of the role of western scientific medicine is offered by J. Powles, 'On the limitations of modern medicine', *Science, Medicine and Man*, vol. 1 no. 1, April 1973; A. L. Cochrane, *Effectiveness and Efficiency in the Health Services*, Nuffield Provincial Hospitals Trust 1972, and T. McKeown, *The Role of Medicine*, Oxford: Basil Blackwell 1979.

See also J. B. McKinlay, 'A case for refocusing upstream: the political economy of sickness', in A. Enelow (ed.) *Applying Behavioural Science to Cardiovascular Risk*, New York: American Heart Association 1975.

Chapter 5.

Specific proposals for an occupational health service have been presented in Socialist Medical Association, *An Occupational Health Service Now*, Birmingham: SMA. The need for a renewed community focus has been argued by T. Heller, *Resstructuring the Health Service*, Croom Helm 1978, and the Unit for the Study of Health Policy, *Rethinking Community Medicine*, Guy's Hospital Medical School 1979. The report of the Black Working Party, *Inequalities in Health*, DHSS 1980, contained a number of specific proposals for development of the health services in these areas. See also P. A. Bertazzi, 'Perspective for environmental surveillance—occupational exposures', in F. Columbo et al (eds.) *Epidemiological Evaluation of Drugs*, Elsevier: North Holland 1977, p. 320; Helen Rosenthal, 'Health and community work—some new approaches', *Radical Community Medicine*, Winter 1980/1, pp. 2–12; *Women and Health—Course Handbook*, Manchester: Trade Union and Basic Education Project, June 1981. B. Inglis, *Fringe Medicine*, Faber and Faber 1964.

Chapter 6.

Details of the formal decision-making structure of the NHS (prior to the removal of the area tier of management in 1982) are given in R. Levitt, *The Reorganised National Health Service*, Croom Helm 1976, and an evaluation of its operation in S. Haywood and A. Alaszewski, *Crisis in the Health Service*, Croom Helm 1980. The purposes of the reorganisation of 1974, in particular its 'managerialist thrust', are examined in P. Draper, G. Grenholm and G. Best, 'The organisation of health care: A critical view of the 1974 reorganisation of the National Health Service', in D. Tuckett (ed.), *An Introduction to Medical Sociology*, Tavistock 1976. Proposals for the development of alternative health plans are contained in the papers prepared for a one-day workshop, Centre for Alternative Industrial and Technological Systems, *Workers Plans for Health*, London: CAITS 1981.

Chapter 7.

A discussion of a broader concept of health is the subject of M. Wilson, *Health is for People*, Darton, Longman & Todd 1975.

The experiences of health and health care in emerging socialist countries have been given in a number of articles in *Medicine in Society*: the Venceremos Brigade, 'Health care in Cuba', *Medicine in Society*, vol. 3 no. 4; K. Gardiner, 'Women and health care in socialist China', *Medicine in Society*, vol. 4 no. 3; M. Segall, 'Health care in liberated Mozambique', *Medicine in Society*, vol. 6 no. 2/3; K. Gardiner, 'Primary care in Cuba', *Medicine in Society*, vol. 7 no. 2/3; A. Hastings, 'Health care in Mozambique', *Medicine in Society*, vol. 7 no. 2/3.

The pamphlet by the Anglo-China Educational Institute, *Health Care in China*, A–CEI 1976, contains an annotated bibliography as well as an article by Joshua Horn, whose autobiographical account, J. Horn, *Away with All Pests*, Monthly Review 1971, remains one of the best testaments on health care in China.

Jenny Beale
Getting It Together

'*I already do two jobs – I'm a worker and a mother. Now you are saying I should do three jobs and be a shop steward as well.*' (June, APEX).

Many things – from sexism to domestic ties to the restrictions of part-time work – hold women back from involvement in trade unions. But when women do join, they enrich trade unionism, bringing strong traditions of action and a powerful challenge to traditional priorities.

Getting It Together examines the overlap between feminist politics and trade unionism and shows that housework and childcare should concern all trade unionists.

Jenny Beale has been a tutor in trade union education and feminist politics for many years. She has written articles on health and safety and many aspects of trades union education.

£2.50   ISBN 0 86104 500 9

Charlie Clutterbuck and Tim Lang
More Than We Can Chew

Under the Common Agricultural Policy, Europe has become a landscape of butter mountains and wine lakes. Farmers produce more food every year. But much of it fails to reach those who need it, a situation that breeds ingenious schemes for dumping and recycling foodstocks.

More Than We Can Chew examines the power struggles and crazy contradictions of the modern world food economy and shows their impact on nutrition, food adulteration and factory conditions.

Charlie Clutterbuck and Tim Lang have both been farmers in the north of England. They are active in the Agricap group of the British Society for Social Responsibility in Science.

£2.50   ISBN 0 86104 501 7

Richard Minns
Take Over the City

In 1982 a row broke out about plans by the Mineworkers' Pension Fund to increase its investments in South Africa. This is just one example of the way a handful of banks, insurance companies and pension funds invest vast sums for short-term gain. They are spending other people's money – savings made through pension schemes, insurance policies and bank accounts. But do decisions made in the City benefit ordinary savers?

The Wilson Committee, set up by the 1974-79 Labour government, found no serious problems with the way the City operates. **Take Over the City** argues differently – that only public ownership of financial institutions can provide the basis for an alternative investment strategy to create jobs.

Richard Minns works for the Economic Development Unit of West Midlands County Council. He is the author of **Pension Funds and British Capitalism.**

£2.50   ISBN 0 86104 502 5